D1267221

LEIBNIZ'S MORAL PHILOSOPHY

LEIBNIZ'S MORAL PHILOSOPHY

John Hostler

BOOKS
10 East 53d St., New York 10022
(a division of Harper & Row Publishers, Inc.)

Published in the U.S.A. 1975 by
HARPER & ROW PUBLISHERS, INC.
BARNES & NOBLE IMPORT DIVISION

© 1975 John Hostler

All rights reserved. No part of this publication
may be reproduced, stored in a retrieval system,
or transmitted, in any form or by any means,
electronic, mechanical, photocopying, recording
or otherwise, without the prior permission of
the copyright owner.

ISBN 0-06-492993-0

Printed in Great Britain by
The Anchor Press Ltd, and bound by
Wm Brendon & Son Ltd, both of Tiptree, Essex

Contents

793006   LIBRARY
          ALMA COLLEGE
          ALMA, MICHIGAN

000067

Preface

The only previous work that deals with the whole of Leibniz's moral philosophy, so far as I know, is Le Chevallier's *La Morale de Leibniz* which appeared in 1933. So many of Leibniz's papers have been published since then that it is necessarily incomplete by modern standards, and therefore little apology needs to be made for producing a new book on the subject.

The present study is based on all the relevant texts so far available, and combines exposition of moral theory with philosophical criticism. It started life as a dissertation submitted for the Ph.D. degree at the University of Cambridge, but I have made substantial changes and amendments in preparing it for publication. I have also translated all quotations into English, in the belief that those readers who are likely to be concerned about nuances of the original will be prepared to look up the references for themselves. I hope that the result of such alterations will serve as an introduction to Leibniz's ethical system for anyone with only the most basic knowledge of his general philosophy; for those wishing to pursue the subject further, the works listed in the Bibliography will be found useful.

I am particularly indebted to Professor Bernard Williams and Dr Ian Hacking, who gave me invaluable help while I was researching and writing the dissertation; to Professor G. H. R. Parkinson and Dr Hidé Ishiguro, who examined it and made many helpful suggestions for its improvement; and above all to my parents, to whom this book is dedicated in gratitude for their constant interest and encouragement.

St Catharine's College, Cambridge   *John Hostler*

Guide to References

The works of Leibniz, and other major sources, are cited by the editions I have used: these are listed at the beginning of the Bibliography, together with their abbreviations. All other works in the Bibliography are numbered, and are referred to in the text by the relevant numeral (in italic type), which may be followed by a page reference. For example, (*37*, 109) would indicate Ahern's *The problem of evil*, page 109.

As a general rule, only one reference is given to substantiate a particular point, and is the clearest or most definite statement of the doctrine in question. Two or more references indicate alternative formulations, differing in presentation or detail.

1   Metaphysical Foundations

Leibniz's theory of ethics has been sadly neglected by most students of his thought. Parts of it have admittedly been discussed in various articles and monographs, but these have generally appeared in recondite journals; while even the best expositions of his philosophy devote only a few pages of superficial comment to his ideas about morality. So the average student, one suspects, will be well acquainted with the elements of his metaphysics and logic, but will probably be quite unaware that he had a moral philosophy besides.

This is a surprising fact, when one considers that the average student can scarcely fail to notice its many manifestations. He has only to pick up the *Discourse on metaphysics* to find, from the second paragraph onwards, a host of arguments about the goodness of God and the moral government of the world; while the *Monadology*, well known as a concise account of Leibniz's metaphysics, ends by recounting the fundamentals of his ethical theory. Indeed, all the more famous works contain frequent allusions to ethical ideas. And even if he has not read them, the student will at least be aware of Leibniz's notorious assertion that this is 'the best of all possible worlds', which carries the explicit moral implications that are discussed in a later chapter.

Yet Leibniz's preoccupation with moral philosophy, thus to be encountered throughout his writings, stems naturally from the course of his philosophical career. Following his father, he trained initially to be a lawyer; and during his years at University and his subsequent employment by the Elector of Mainz, he produced no less than twelve substantial works on the theory of law and ethics. So that when he moved to Paris in 1672, at the age of 26, there to begin his brilliant work on mathematics, logic and metaphysics, he had already developed the essentials of his whole moral system. He continued with its development right until his death in 1716. This was partly because it always

remained his chief interest : at the beginning of the *New Essays*
of 1704, for instance, he assesses himself vis-à-vis Locke by commenting that 'you are more in the tradition of metaphysical
thought, whereas I am more interested in ethics' (A.vi.vi.71).
And partly, it was because he regarded the divers subjects of
his enquiries as interconnected. This is revealed in a letter of
1679, in which he has just described his plans for future work on
theology :

> To lay the foundations for this great work, and to make it
> intelligible, I plan first to establish the *Elements* of true
> philosophy. For we need a new *logic*, to assess degrees of
> probability . . . We must make considerable advances in
> *metaphysics*, to have true concepts of God and the soul, of
> persons, and of substance and accident. Unless we have a
> more basic knowledge of *physics* we shall not be able to cope
> with the problems attending the story of the creation, the
> flood, and the resurrection of bodies. And finally we must
> discover the true theory of *ethics* to understand the nature
> of justice, justification, freedom, pleasure and happiness.
> (A.II.i.489)

The work for which Leibniz has subsequently become famous was
thus intimately connected, in his own mind, with his endeavours
to develop the 'true' theory of ethics. Since, as we have seen, he
did not properly commence that work until his ethical theory
was largely complete, one may reasonably expect it to show signs
of an ulterior, ethical purpose. This is indeed the case. His
system of metaphysics in particular can be seen, in many respects,
as providing a conceptual framework for the system of morals,
and thus it provides a convenient starting-point for this discussion.

Leibniz, as is well known, believed the universe to comprise an
infinite number of 'monads'. These monads are the only real
substances, and each of them is an indivisible point of force, a
union of an active and a passive principle called 'entelechy' and
'primary matter' respectively.[1] The monad is generally described

---

1. Hacking (57) has argued that the Leibnizian monad has an important
similarity with what we might be prepared to call a 'substance' because of
these principles of action and passion. He points out that material objects

in spiritual terms : it is like a 'self' in its essential unity, it has no material extension, and its activity consists in an unending series of impressions and ideas that succeed one another according to 'laws' of appetition or desire. Leibniz is prone to describe these ideas as 'perceptions', which is unfortunately misleading since they do not depend upon there being anything to 'perceive'. He asserts that the monad would still have them even if everything were destroyed but God and itself (Gr.299, E.127): so it is safest to understand them as pure mental images, not dependent upon outside sources for their origin, but arising from within the monad itself.

This metaphysical conception thus entails the paradox of solipsism, since the monad 'has no windows' and is like 'a world apart'. It also entails the paradox of immaterialism, since the only true existents are minds. Both of these paradoxes are overcome by Leibniz's doctrine of the 'pre-established harmony', which states that there is a perfect and regular correspondence between all the monads' impressions. Not only does this permit us to say that a monad 'expresses' the existence and activity of its fellows in its impressions (G.II.12); it also allows a certain reality to be attributed to matter and motion, as Leibniz, mindful of the arguments in Descartes' first *Meditation*, explains :

---

can be said (rather loosely) to 'do' things or have things 'done' to them, and this is closely connected with our readiness to regard them as distinct elements of the physical world. One should also note that Aristotle claims that substances are differentiated by ostensive definition: he observes that action and passion merely constitute the nature of substance, and that one is distinguished from another by the fact that each is a 'this' (*10*, 1001b).

Leibniz clearly agrees about the attributes of action and passion, but must disagree with Aristotle about the possibility of ostensive definition. He writes that 'spirits, minds, and simple substances or monads in general, cannot be comprehended by sense or imagination since they have no parts' (E.678). This derives from his initial premiss that substance is essentially indivisible; for since a 'material atom' is 'contrary to reason' (G.IV.482 – for matter can always be divided), it follows that all substances must be spiritual. The fact that they cannot be 'comprehended' perhaps accounts for his thesis that every substance involves infinity in itself, which will be seen to be of great importance in Chapter 4.

It must be observed that Leibniz is using the word 'entelechy' in a peculiar sense. For him, it connotes a capability to become perfect: for Aristotle, it originally meant an achieved state of being perfect.

Their 'reality' lies only in the agreement between the monads' impressions. If things happened exactly according to the dreams of an individual, and if the dreams of every other mind also agreed with them, that would be entirely sufficient to constitute body and matter. (G.ɪɪɪ.567)

His point here is that physical bodies, though strictly they are mere 'phenomena', are none the less 'well-founded' phenomena : they are not illusions, as their behaviour must always correspond with our impressions of it – since, at the metaphysical level, their behaviour is simply a matter of correspondence between our impressions. In this fashion, therefore, Leibniz is enabled to use subjective experience to create an objective reality.

Accordingly he maintains that 'the ordinary ways of talking are preserved intact', despite his unusual premises (E.128). He himself speaks, for instance, of God as creating the monads at different viewpoints of the world (G.ɪv.439), though in fact the world has no existence apart from these constituent 'views'. More importantly for his ethics, he can claim that every monad has a body, and that his theory of the pre-established harmony provides an effective solution to the problem of interaction between mind and body that had so baffled Descartes (E.127); indeed, the problem disappears, since body is basically analysable in terms of mind. However, Leibniz generally treats mind and body as distinct entities. He points out that it is the nature of mind to be self-moving, and of body to be moved by something else (Gr.299); and consequently maintains that their activity is to be explained differently, in terms of reasons and causes respectively.

The maintenance of this view clearly depends upon a distinction between the concepts of reason and cause which, it is sometimes claimed, he fails to provide. It is true that he seems to regard the terms *causa* and *ratio* as synonymous on occasion, as when he treats as equivalent the two principles 'nothing happens without a cause, or there is nothing without a reason' (G.vɪɪ.301). But at other times he distinguishes them sharply, as when he writes that 'a cause is an extrinsic reason, a reason for the production of something : but a reason can be intrinsic to the thing itself' (Gr.13). An important example of such intrinsic reasons occurs with necessary truths, where one can see the reason why they are necessarily true but would hesitate to call it a 'cause', which is a term more appropriately applied to the realm of actual physical events. Thus Leibniz suggests, in effect, that the distinction between reasons and causes coincides with that between necessary and contingent truths – a criterion that is at least as clear as any other that has been proposed. The suspicion that he confused the concepts would seem to stem from his metaphysics rather than his definitions. We find that Spinoza, too, had used the terms synonymously (S.1.44); yet this was because a central feature of his metaphysical theory is the exact parallelism of Thought and Extension, which carries the consequence that every event has both a cause and a reason that are like the two sides of a single coin. Leibniz's thought involves a very similar result. His analysis of body in terms of the correspondence between the monads' experiences implies that any instance of physical movement can be explained either in terms of internal mental activity, or as the effect of external dynamic impulse.

Although recognising that either form of explanation could thus suffice by itself (G.VI.542), he insists that they should both be retained since they are best suited to different kinds of activity. Contrary to expectation, however, he is not thinking here of the activity of mind and body, but rather of those monads that are endowed with reason and of those that are not (C.329). For only some monads can behave rationally : these are called 'spirits', while the others, devoid of reason, are called 'beasts'. This division is justified by the fact that rational and non-rational behaviour demand different forms of explanation. At C.20, for instance, he observes that the spirits' capacity for purposive action renders their behaviour unpredictable to an observer, and is best accounted for in terms of their intentions and motives, in which respect they are fundamentally similar to God. The activity of the beasts, however, can properly be explained by means of efficient causes : a view that implies a quasi-Cartesian understanding of animals as extremely complex machines (e.g., A.VI.i.466).

It needs to be observed that there is a very definite tension between this classification of the monads and the conception that was aptly named by Lovejoy 'the Great Chain of Being'. For Leibniz asserts repeatedly that the monads are arranged in

a 'continuum', differing only by infinitesimal degrees; arguing
that any gap or break in this 'chain', any *vacuum formarum*,
would be inadmissible in the best of all possible worlds (G.vi.
543). On the other hand, he also maintains that there are important differences between the monads regarding the degree of clarity and connection of their experiences. At G.ii.112, for example,
he claims that a series of impressions such as every monad has
can take the form of bare awareness, of sensory perception, or
of intellectual understanding, thus restating the threefold
division of mental activity made earlier by Aristotle (*11*, 413b).
Although the continuum and its divisions are theoretically compatible, it seems that they are not fully harmonised in Leibniz's
thought.[2] He attaches great significance to the fact that the
behaviour of spirits and beasts is subject to different laws; and it
is noteworthy that whereas Aquinas, who held a similar opinion,
had regarded such laws as related species of a higher 'eternal
law' (ST.i.aiiae 91,2), Leibniz adopts no such means of
softening the distinction :

> Though every substance represents the whole universe [in its
> experience], we can say that the beasts represent more of the
> world than of God, while the spirits represent more of God
> than the world. So God governs the beasts in accordance
> with the material laws of force and mechanics; but he
> governs the spirits in accordance with the spiritual laws of
> justice, which are not applicable to the others. (G.ii.124)

The most important difference between the spirits and beasts,
however, concerns the manner in which they survive after death.

2. Leibniz defines the concept as follows: 'A continuum is a whole of
which the parts are without parts, and indeterminate. They are "without
parts" in the sense that they can be perceived separately; and in this, it is
distinguished from a "gradual whole" whose parts run into one another'
(C.438). As such, a continuum can easily involve an apparent sharp
division. An example is that suggested by Ian Hacking, of a series of
arithmetical fractions running from a point less than unity to one greater
than it.
　All the same, this does not really exempt Leibniz from criticism. It is
not simply that some monads in the series are rational while others are not,
as some fractions are less than unity: this difference is made the basis for a
radical division of the universe into two realms. It seems a weak foundation
for such a strong claim.

As a true substance, it is of course impossible that any monad should cease to exist, unless through deliberate annihilation by God. Leibniz had deduced this from the essential indivisibility of the monad, employing the premiss that all destruction involves a 'dissolution of parts' (E.464); but one may note that he could also have argued from its essential activity, as Plato had done (*Phaedrus*, 245c). Either way, the monad exists eternally, and repeatedly passes through a cycle : at 'death', the animal suffers a fragmentation of its gross body and a consequent confusion in its perceptions, while at 'birth' an increase in the clarity of its experience is accompanied by the re-acquisition of an organic body. Lest we should be confused by the similarity between this idea and the theories of Plato and Pythagoras, Leibniz warns us that 'there is no Metempsychosis, only Metamorphosis' (G.vi.601): making the crucial point that the monad is always embodied, so that it is the animal, and not the soul alone, that continues always to exist. For the spirits, however, things are very different indeed. In the first place, we learn that the rational soul is not eternally existent, but is created when its body is formed (G.ii.75): in other words, the monad that is to become a spirit pre-exists without reason, and receives an infusion of rationality from God at the moment when the human embryo is conceived – a 'supernatural accretion' that transforms it into a spirit (Gr.552). This exceptional process is matched by the manner of the spirits' survival after death. Although, like the other monads, their material bodies suffer dissolution and decay (G.ii.325), their experience is not subject to the same degree of disruption : 'death' is no more than a brief and confused dream for them, from which they will eventually awake with continued sense, reason and self-consciousness (G.vi.522).

Leibniz's assertion of these doctrines is remarkable for the fact that they are supported by moral arguments alone : specifically, by the premiss that the spirits must receive due reward and punishment from God. It is for this reason, he says, that the spirits alone are able to feel pleasure and pain (A.vi.i.466). For this reason too, they retain memory and self-consciousness :

> For it is memory, or knowledge of one's *self*, that permits both punishment and reward. The sort of immortality that is needed in morality and religion is not the endless existence

possessed by every substance, for that is entirely useless without the memory of one's past. (G.IV.460)

One can see that this is an entirely valid assertion. The punishment of a man who cannot remember his criminal actions presents a peculiar ethical problem, since he will not understand the pain we may inflict upon him *as* punishment unless we can first convince him that he is guilty of his crimes. If we fail in this, he will not know what the pain is *for*; unlike the man who believes himself to be innocent, and therefore regards it as punishment that is simply unjust. For similar reasons, punishment requires an awareness of one's 'self'. If a man's experiences were as chaotic and confused as those of the lower monads, he might well feel pain without realising that it was *he* who was suffering, as a discrete and conscious individual. The spirits therefore, as Leibniz asserts, must retain both memory and self-consciousness, and these two together constitute what he calls their 'moral identity' (G.V.218). This concept is to be distinguished from that of the purely metaphysical identity of the monad, which is discussed in a later chapter.

It is apparent from this brief survey that Leibniz's metaphysical system, at even its most fundamental level, thus has a definite ethical purpose. The basic homogeneity of the monads is quite overshadowed by what he admits to be 'the vast difference' between the spirits and beasts (E.464): a difference that hinges solely upon the possession of reason, but is nevertheless extended to cover the explanation of behaviour, the possession of mental attributes, and the whole manner of existence. So important is this difference that it divides the single universe of monads into two distinct parts, called the 'Realm of Nature' and the 'Realm of Grace'. Each of these 'realms' or 'kingdoms' is precisely what the name implies – a number of individuals, co-existing together, whose behaviour is governed by a set of laws. In the realm of nature are all the non-rational monads, whose activity is subject to the contingent laws of physics and is best explained in terms of cause and effect. In the realm of grace are all the monads with reason; and though they are also subject to the laws of physics, their deliberate and voluntary conduct is best explained in terms of reasons and intentions, and is recompensed by God in accordance with the necessary laws of morality. Most importantly, the realm of nature is subordinate to it :

> This society, or universal Republic of Spirits under their sovereign Monarch, is the most noble part of the universe. It is composed of lesser gods beneath the great God, for one can say that the created spirits differ from God only in degree, as finite from infinite. It is certainly true, besides, that the universe as a whole has been created simply to add to the glory and happiness of this divine city. (G.II.125)

As Friedmann has observed (59, 247), the priority between these two realms appears as an established feature of Leibniz's philosophy as early as 1671. It is therefore hardly surprising to find, as we have done, that the initial simplicity and homogeneity of his metaphysical system is largely sacrificed in favour of this division between the two kinds of monad. Nor is it surprising, as we have also seen, that the only arguments adduced in its support are ethical ones : for in 1670 Leibniz had already announced his firm intention of establishing a proper sort of immortality, such as he claims for the spirits, as one of the necessary foundations of morality (A.II.i.29). It is clear that the realm of grace is expressly designed as a framework within which to develop a theory of ethics, since it satisfies all the requirements of the moral world : it contains discrete individuals, endowed with the capacity for deliberate action and for receiving reward and punishment, and subject to a code of moral law. It is not a particularly novel idea : the theories of Plotinus and many Stoic philosophers, for instance, anticipate it in most fundamental respects. But it serves Leibniz's purposes admirably well, as we shall see in due course.

2   Action and Volition

Aristotle seems to have been the first philosopher to assert that some internal process of decision is necessarily involved in all voluntary action (*10*, 1048a). This idea was developed into the concept of a 'faculty' of soul by Scholastic thinkers and transmitted by them to the seventeenth century, when Leibniz, together with his contemporaries, accepted the dogma that 'the will' is an essential element in human action. However, it was the term alone that was thus accepted without question, since we find many different views of what it denotes. According to Leibniz, whose view will be seen to be unique in many respects, 'the will is a striving (*conatus*) that follows the agent's judgment (*opinio*) of good or evil' (Gr.513).

Let us first examine these elements of *conatus* and *opinio*. Probably because he derived his theories from a long philosophical tradition, Leibniz has very little to say about his analysis of volition, and we therefore have to depend upon a number of scattered remarks for explanation. A typical one is found at RI.60, where he observes that just as physical events occur through motion according to the laws of dynamics, 'so, in the mind, everything happens through this striving, through desire in accordance with the laws of value'. This suggests that *conatus* constitutes the very essence of mind, and that one is to understand the internal activity of a spirit in terms of an unceasing desire. This interpretation is confirmed by his statement at G.vii.330 that the perceptions of a primitive monad arise through simple appetition, to which there corresponds a conscious will in the case of rational spirits. One can therefore deny the claim of Naert (*101*) and Russell (*116*), among others, that Leibniz derived his notion of *conatus* from Hobbes. For Hobbes had defined 'endeavour' as 'motion made in an instant of time' (*De corpore*, 15); whereas Leibniz not only denied that motion has any substantial reality, as we have already seen, but even contrasts mind and body in this respect, saying that 'thought consists in striving, as body consists in motion' (G.i.47). The only point of similarity, indeed, lies in the fact that Leibniz and Hobbes both thought of the will as producing motion of itself, thus differing from the earlier view of will as a 'faculty', understood as a mere capacity to be moved. For Leibniz the *conatus* is a mental activity, functioning as a source of motion but not itself being moved.

The other element in volition is the judgment (*opinio*) that precedes and directs the desire. Leibniz laid stress upon this in conscious opposition to other philosophers, especially Descartes – who had maintained that the human will could operate at times without the intellect, and that in the case of God it was not even possible to distinguish them (AT.i.153). Leibniz vehemently opposed these Cartesian views, maintaining that the divine and human will alike presuppose a reason for volition, as otherwise it would be a matter of 'blind chance' (G.vii.390). Unfortunately, he is less explicit about the nature or content of this all-important judgment. There seem to be only two comments that give a clue to it : the first at C.283, where he says that one understands that something *is* the case but wills that it *should be* so; and the second at A.vi.i.284, where he claims that 'willing is simply judging the goodness of something'. Clearly, these statements conflict : the first claims that the judgment is prescriptive, while the second asserts that it is categorical in form. The only way these can be reconciled is to suppose that the judgment is in fact an inference, of the form 'since X is good, it should be done', which includes both the value-judgment and the prescription of action.

This suggested interpretation acquires greater plausibility when one observes its similarity to the views of Aristotle, since Leibniz agrees with him in many respects. Aristotle certainly believed that the deliberation which precedes action can be cast in standard logical form, his so-called doctrine of the 'practical syllogism' (EN.1142b); and the inference sketched above clearly represents the minor premiss and conclusion of a syllogism in Darii. Similarly, Leibniz agrees with Aristotle that desire and judgment are of equal importance in volition. It would be entirely possible for a man not to do what he believes should be done, because he is feeling lazy or uncooperative, for example;

but when he wants to do it as well, this is unlikely to happen. Therefore, as Leibniz's definition suggests, the judgment merely directs the desire, which is already present in an independent capacity. His view is thus again the same as that expressed in Aristotle's comment, that 'our judgment comes from deliberation, while our desire accords with it' (EN.1113a). Though the precedence of reason over desire is therefore merely logical rather than temporal, it nevertheless carries the important implication for Leibnizian ethics that correct judgment should always result in right action.

Leibniz's cheerful acceptance of 'the will' as an essential part of voluntary action may well prove a stumbling-block to those readers who are acquainted with Ryle's forceful criticisms of it as an absurd and unintelligible hypothesis, involving an infinite regress of 'acts of will' (*117*, 62 ff.). It is therefore important to observe that Ryle's strictures have no application to the theories of Leibniz – nor, indeed, to those of his major contemporaries and successors, so far as I can discover. The kind of theory that Ryle attacks is found only in the works of very minor philosophers. One such is the little-known Jacob Thomasius who, in the tenth 'table' of his work (*29*), sets out a scheme of incredible complexity in which the will is pictured as a distinct psychological entity, endowed with a liberty of its own, and arbitrating the rival claims of reason and desire. Such a scheme certainly involves an infinite regress; likewise, the absurdities of an 'act of will' are evident in the distinction between 'elicited' and 'commanded' acts of volition that Thomasius attempts to maintain.[3] His signifi-

3. Thomasius defines the ideas as follows:

Elicited: what the will immediately achieves by itself, or what is elicited from within the will itself – such as wishing, declining, choosing or rejecting.
Commanded: what the will achieves indirectly, what is done by other powers (the sensitive and locomotive appetites) at the order of the will. An example is eating. (*29*, tab. 10)

The 'act of will' is the first of these two: when an action is performed, the will first wills to will it and then wills to do it. Ryle's argument depends on the fact that the theory is intended to explain the occurrence of voluntary action. Simply put, it says that the elicited act must be voluntary or involuntary: if the latter, then the physical act must also be involuntary; but if voluntary, then by parity of reasoning there should be a further elicited act to account for it, whence the vicious regress arises.

cance for the present discussion lies in the fact that he was
Professor at the University of Leipzig; and since the first edition
of his book appeared in 1661, the year that Leibniz began his
studies there, it is reasonable to suppose that it was made his
standard textbook. It is therefore greatly to Leibniz's credit that
he never accepted any of its ridiculous schemes, but rather
anticipated Ryle's chief criticism by observing that a vicious
regress would be generated if 'the will' had 'a mind of its own'
as suggested (E.643). Leibniz's own theory, it must be empha-
sised, is simple and largely free from difficulties. For him, volition
is no more than 'thinking about good and evil, conjoined with
a desire to act' (Gr.14).

The 'object' of volition, in the sense of its aim or end, is taken
by Leibniz to be 'the good'. This again was a largely traditional
doctrine, and many agreed that 'the good' was equivalent, at
least in the majority of cases, to 'what the agent seeks to do'
(A.vi.ii.493). Opinion was divided, however, on the point that
had been raised first by Plato (*Euthyphro*, 10a), as to whether
a thing should be called 'good' because it is willed, or whether
it is willed because it is known to be good. Both Spinoza
(S.iii.204) and Hobbes (R.4) had adopted the former alternative; but Leibniz accepted the latter doctrine, as indeed one
might expect from the emphasis he lays upon the importance of
judgment in volition. If the label is not misleading, he may be
described as an 'objectionist', in the sense that he believes the
goodness of something to depend on criteria other than the fact
of its being willed, desired or chosen.

There are, in fact, two such criteria. The one that he
mentions most frequently is the extent to which an object is
pleasant: 'the good is what contributes to pleasure' (Gr.11).
Taking this as the defining characteristic of goodness, he divides
good things into two classes: those which are 'pleasant' in themselves, and those which are 'useful' as a means to obtaining
them (ibid.). He also makes another distinction of greater

The argument clearly does not apply to Leibniz's synthesis of reason and
desire. Neither, it should be observed, does it apply to the English philosophers such as Hobbes and Locke, even though they sometimes speak of an
'act of will' in their works. They are using the phrase in the sense in which
it might be contrasted with 'act of habit': it merely expresses the idea of
deliberate voluntary action.

importance, between 'internal' and 'external' goods : the former, as he says at Gr.96, arise 'from within ourselves', while the latter are generally regarded as 'a matter of luck'. This distinction seems to have been misunderstood by Schiedermair, who takes an external good to be something that produces pleasure, and an internal good to be the pleasure itself (*118*, 30) : for Leibniz claims at M.62 that wisdom and virtue are essentially good – and these are not only 'internal' in the sense he has defined, but are just as productive of pleasure as external circumstances. Indeed, he agrees on this point with Thomasius, who maintains that neither kind of good is to be identified with pleasure itself (*29*, tab. 3). This view, that goods are always things that *produce* pleasure, will be seen later to be of crucial importance.

Leibniz makes yet a third distinction, between 'real' and 'apparent' goods. He describes it as a 'very ancient' doctrine (C.25), having in mind perhaps the views of Aquinas (ST.ıaııae, 26.4), or more probably those of Aristotle (EN.1155b). However, what Aristotle has to say is extremely ambiguous; and one finds that even in the seventeenth century the same division of terms is used to express two different doctrines. The first of these takes the two descriptions – 'the real good' and 'the apparent good' – to be mutually exclusive, denying that they can both be applied to the same object. Thomasius, for instance, writes that 'the apparent good is in fact not good but bad' (*29*, n. 11). Leibniz, however, adopts the second doctrine, which does not involve any incompatibility between the two descriptions. It asserts that something is an apparent good if it is believed to produce pleasure, and a real good if it actually does produce pleasure. The difference between seeking the apparent and the real good is therefore largely a matter of success : it is only when the agent's real good *appears* good to him that he will attain the pleasure he desires. According to Leibniz, this fortunate state of affairs is guaranteed only for the wise man, it being the function of knowledge to discover the 'real' goods, the things that can be rationally desired by someone who has complete knowledge of all the relevant factors.

Although this emphasis on wisdom is an important consequence, attention must also be paid to the fact that there is a necessary connection between the apparent good and volition. For Leibniz writes that 'nothing is desired by us unless it appears to be good' (C.25). This reveals that the apparent good is what would be called in Scholastic terminology the 'formal object' of the will; or, in the modern phrase, it is the 'description under which' things must fall if they are to be objects of volition. This is supposedly based upon an analytic relationship, since Leibniz assumes that it is part of the very meaning of 'willing' an action that the agent regards it as good; thus he says that anything can be called good 'in a way', inasmuch as someone wills it (A.vi.i.458). We can therefore see that the difference between the apparent and real good is coincident with that between description and prescription. The apparent good is what the agent *does* will, while the real good is what he *should* do.

As the first criterion of goodness is thus pleasure, so the second is introduced by its analysis. Leibniz writes : 'I think that pleasure is basically a sensation of perfection, and pain one of imperfection, of a sufficient intensity for one to be conscious of it' (A.vi.vi.194). The concept of perfection mentioned here is of such complexity, and of such general significance for the whole of Leibniz's ethical system, that it will be dealt with fully in a later chapter. For the present, we need to observe only two points. The first is that when he speaks of pleasure as being an awareness of perfection, what Leibniz means is that one perceives an increase in perfection. He writes, for instance, that 'I give the name "perfection" to all improvement (*Erhöhung*) in being' (E.672); and, more explicitly, 'pleasure is the awareness of increasing perfection' (M.88). The philosophical significance of this lies in its anticipation of the views of MacIntyre, who has argued cogently that pleasure is not a simple sensation like pain, but the consciousness of an essentially dynamic process that accompanies activity (92, 216). This theory is clearly inherent in Leibniz's analysis of pleasure.

The second point to be noticed is that Leibniz offers no justification for his definition : he has no arguments to show *why* the perception of increased perfection should be pleasant. This might seem surprising, and possibly a fatal weakness in his theories. But it should be observed that both Spinoza and Descartes likewise associated pleasure with perfection, without providing any justification; while Kant included in his ethical theory the premiss that we derive pleasure from the consciousness of virtuous action, and yet maintained that there was no possible explanation for this (K.iv.460). Such comparisons suggest that Leibniz's definition of pleasure should be regarded as a fundamental postulate of his philosophy, and not as a conclusion derived from other theories. Indeed, it is difficult to see how such a doctrine could be supported. It seems to be a brute fact that some things are pleasant while others are not; and while the moral philosopher must take this into account, it is not clear that he is obliged to provide an explanation for it. One may wish, therefore, that Leibniz had stated explicitly that his definition of pleasure is a postulate, but it would be unfair to condemn his theory because it is not otherwise explained.

The two criteria of 'the good', then, are as follows : it is that which produces pleasure, and that which contributes to increased perfection. Which of these criteria is primary? This question is of considerable importance, since the answer to it determines the whole character of Leibniz's ethical theory. If the production of pleasure is primary, perfection being mentioned simply as a weak explanation of that, his theory will be fundamentally hedonistic; and since only the spirits can feel pleasure, as we have seen in the previous chapter, it will be anthropocentric as well. On the other hand, if the criterion of perfection is primary and pleasure is merely its manifestation to rational souls, his theory will be basically naturalistic, and the particular values of morality will be founded upon a universal, metaphysical scheme of value. Leibniz gives us no definite answer to this question, but certain passages suggest that his theory fits the second model. At Gr.15, for instance, he deduces the value of a thing from its perfection, and uses his theory of pleasure merely as a premiss in the argument. And at G.iii.32 he defines three distinct kinds of goodness : 'metaphysical' good is perfection in general, and includes the good of non-rational monads; 'physical' good is pleasure itself; and 'moral' good is virtuous action, to which pleasure accrues (a definition to be compared with Locke's, as the conformity of action to a law whereby reward is gained, at R.138). Such comments seem to show that the real scheme of value is based upon perfection, and that the spirits' perception of this as pleasure is merely a part of the whole.

If Leibniz's analysis of value is fundamentally naturalistic, as it thus appears to be, it will be asked whether he does not commit the 'naturalistic fallacy' – defined by Moore as taking the word 'good' to be equivalent in meaning with one or more 'natural', or non-evaluative terms (99, 10 ff.). Again, of course, Leibniz fails to anticipate such sophisticated queries. But a defence against the charge can probably be constructed from his comments in the thirteenth section of the *Discourse on metaphysics*, where he maintains that it is an entirely contingent fact that 'a man will do what appears best to him' (G.iv.438). When this observation is set alongside the statement we have noted earlier, that 'the good' is the object of volition, he would appear to be saying that the association of value with pleasure and perfection is merely contingent : in other words, it just happens to be the case that we will what appears pleasant, and this might not be so in some other scheme of things. If this is his meaning, he clearly does not believe that 'good' necessarily *means* the same as 'pleasant'; though, by a fortunate decree of God, they happen to be co-extensive terms. This interpretation is strengthened by the following passage, in which our search after pleasure is conceived as a (contingent) law of nature :

> Man inclines towards pleasant things as a stone falls towards the centre [of the earth]. But happiness is the kind of pleasure that right reason bids us seek : pleasure that endures, and does not lead subsequently to greater miseries. This could not be made the object of our inclinations as an immediate and general rule, any more than it could be ordained that the stone should always take the optimal path to the centre, and not be broken by collisions on its way. (Gr.487)

This quotation reminds us again of the distinction between desire and reason in volition; and asserts that the latter element is essential for our achievement of happiness, the true end for man, since desire seeks only immediate pleasures while 'reason directs us to the future and enduring pleasure' (A.vi.vi.90). Nevertheless, the element of desire is also of great importance, for this is the basis of a doctrine that is crucial to Leibniz's ethical system – namely, that every deliberate action of mine is directed to the attainment of *my own* good (A.i.vi.198). Such fundamental egoism had been a feature of earlier philosophy too: Aquinas, for instance, had written that all voluntary acts are performed 'because they are beneficial to the agent himself' (SP.III.3). But neither Aquinas nor Leibniz can mean that all my actions must *really* be beneficial to me, since that would remove all possibility of error; nor even that they must *appear* to be so, since I may well drink alcohol in full knowledge of its harmful effects. The solution to this problem is reached by analysing the nature of desire. The statement 'I desire X' implies at least two subsidiary propositions: that 'what I desire is X', and 'I expect some pleasure from getting X'. This point was noticed by Descartes, who observes that the 'end' of our actions is both our ultimate good and the happiness that comes from its possession (AT.IV.275). The point to be observed, however, is that the pleasure which I anticipate is necessarily my own. Because he has defined the good as that which is pleasant, Leibniz thus means that *my* good is simply what is pleasant for me; and he maintains that it is always the object of my volitions because desire is an integral element in the will.

One must here bear in mind the point made earlier, that 'the good' is not the same as pleasure itself. If this were not so, Leibniz would be bound to maintain that the object of my volition is the pleasure I anticipate from getting X, and not X itself: in which case, altruistic behaviour would be impossible. He would have made the mistake that Butler attacks so fiercely (R.416), and which has since been named the fallacy of 'egoistic hedonism' by Von Wright, and described by him as mistaking 'the necessary connection, which holds between the satisfaction of desire and pleasure, for a necessary connection between desire and pleasure *as its object*' (*128*, 83). As things are, however, Leibniz carefully avoids this pitfall. He maintains that my acts must offer some pleasure to me; but he leaves open the possibility that they may be pleasant to others as well, which is clearly of great significance from the standpoint of his moral philosophy.

There is one final problem to be discussed. It has been argued that if I desire something I expect it to be pleasant; but does my belief that something will be pleasant imply that I must desire it? Leibniz, as we have seen, does not maintain that my desire is always caused by such a belief, since he restricts the element of judgment to a purely guiding role. On the other hand, there clearly ought to be some fairly regular correspondence, as otherwise it would be quite possible for me never to want to do the things I judged to be good. Both Plato (*Philebus*, 20d) and Spinoza (S.I.194) maintained that I *must* desire what I judge to be good; and while Leibniz rejects this extreme doctrine, his association of value with pleasure permits a certain regularity to be established. MacIntyre, for instance, has pointed out a close link between finding an activity pleasant and wanting to do it again (92, 225); while Anscombe has argued that though it is possible for me not to want something that I judge myself to need, it is not possible for me *never* to want it (75, 182). This remains true even when 'thinking pleasant' is substituted for 'needing'. If we encountered a man who never had any desire for something he judged to be pleasant, we would conclude either that he did not know the meaning of 'pleasant', or that he was psychologically lacking in some respect. Inasmuch as Leibniz associates a judgment of value with the expectation of pleasure, we can therefore conclude that, as a general rule, the belief that something is good will tend to be linked with a desire to obtain it : and this is probably quite adequate for his purposes. We need to note only one important exception to this rule, namely, that it is quite possible to approve the actions of others 'where there is no room for our election', as Hutcheson puts it (R.358). In terms of the Leibnizian analysis, I may well believe that your action is good without wishing to behave likewise, since I can merely hold that it is pleasant for you.

Leibniz's account of the will is very intimately linked with his analysis of the value of its objects, and this has made it impossible to separate the various strands of his theory as much as would have been desirable. We can now, however, identify five fundamental propositions that constitute the main points of the theory, which may be stated as follows :

1. The good is that which produces pleasure.
2. Pleasure is the perception of an increase in perfection.
3. Volition is desire governed by judgment.
4. The judgment is always of an apparent good.
5. The desire is always for one's own good.

These propositions are set out here not merely for the reader's convenience, or to clarify the previous discussion. For it will be seen in due course that the whole of Leibniz's ethical system is constructed in accordance with them, and indeed that several of its constituent doctrines are deduced from them alone. They thus form a conceptual framework for his moral philosophy that is of the greatest significance.

3 Freewill and Determinism

The most common ground for attack upon Leibniz's ethical system surely centres upon the question of freewill. It has been argued by many that several of his theories cast the possibility of free action into jeopardy, and that since he conspicuously fails to solve the problems thus arising his moral philosophy is doomed from the outset. Accordingly, in this chapter and the next, we shall examine the adequacy of his proposed solutions; concentrating on the problems generated by his own theories, since his treatment of various traditional issues is the subject of a fine study by Parkinson (*104*). We shall begin with the problems arising from his theory of volition itself.

It has been shown in the previous chapter that the will consists of desire that is, for most practical purposes, subject to the rational judgment. The threat to freedom comes not from this, but from the thesis that the judgment itself is also subject to determination. Such an idea had been championed by Hobbes; he makes it the basis for one of his objections to the *Meditations* of Descartes, who does not properly refute it in his reply (AT.ix. 149); and Leibniz too, in his observations upon Hobbes' work, is forced to agree that our volitions are not 'in our power' to the same extent as our actions (E.630). For, as we can see, the value of an object is claimed to be a function of its degree of perfection, and therefore the agent has no choice as to whether a thing is good or bad since its value is wholly independent of his opinions. The 'judgment' in volition, in fact, does not involve decision so much as recognition of the truth. This is clearly expressed in the following passage :

> It is true that we possess spontaneity, and that we choose what we wish; but we wish for what we find to be good : and that depends upon our taste and the objects, not upon our choice. And when through fancy, or perhaps to demon-

strate our liberty, we choose something that we would otherwise regard as bad, it is because the pleasure that comes from
acting in this unusual way is made a part of the object, and
because our spirit of rebellion forms a part of our taste.
(Gr.482)

This idea of 'taste' is an important and intriguing aspect of
Leibniz's theory. It can best be explained by another of his
theories, that of the distinction between antecedent and consequent will, which had initially been developed by the Church
Fathers to cope with the theological problem of evil. Leibniz,
however, frequently presents it in purely general terms, and it
appears to have formed an integral part of his account of human
action. Briefly, it states that when we are considering a course of
action, especially one course among many, the will is first
attracted or repelled as the various elements and alternatives
are seen to be good or bad in isolation – these are the antecedent
volitions; then these initial apprehensions are combined to
produce a single consequent volition, which results in the performance of the eventual act (G.vi.170, Gr.502). The process
can be seen as analogous to that of the resolution of forces in
dynamics, for it carries the same implication that the resulting
impulse is determined by its various constituents. Now the element
of 'taste' seems to be related to, if not wholly identical with, the
antecedent volitions, since Leibniz uses the term to describe one's
disposition to choose in certain ways, as a result of internal
characteristics that (logically) precede and determine the choice
eventually made. We can understand it as 'weighting' the
antecedent volitions more or less, so that some of them will have
greater influence than others. Leibniz certainly intends it to be
the counterpart of Aristotle's notion of *hexis*, which similarly
helps to determine whether something is regarded as good or
bad (EN.1114).

The role of dispositions in the determination of volition is
reinforced by Leibniz's comment that they include, besides
conscious reasons, mere 'inclinations' that are the result of previous experience. This is a reference to his famous theory of
'minute perceptions' – experiences of which we are not aware,
but which nevertheless have a definite effect upon the mind.
This recognition of the influence of the unconscious mind is

probably the most remarkable of Leibniz's psychological ideas. These perceptions play an important part in his theory of volition since, even though we are not aware of them, 'they often enter into the practical judgments of the intellect' (G.vi.300). Most importantly, they determine all actions that are not the result of conscious deliberation. For instance, they cause me to put one foot first rather than the other when I leave a room (G.vi.128); and when, tossing a coin, I decide 'without thinking' which of the alternatives is to be represented by 'heads' or 'tails', this choice too is unconsciously determined by preceding inclinations (Gr.488).

It is generally held to be an objection to all determinist accounts of volition that there exist cases of *akrasia*, when an agent fails to adopt in practice what he sincerely judges to be the best course of action. Leibniz's treatment of such cases is of the utmost significance, and is typically expressed in the following passage:

When God makes a choice, it is through his knowledge of the best; when man does so, he will choose the alternative that seems to be best. If, nevertheless, he chooses what appears less useful or pleasant, it will probably have come to seem the most attractive because of a whim, a spirit of contradiction, or similar reasons of his corrupt taste – reasons that still determine his choice, even though they would not otherwise be valid. There are no exceptions to this rule. (G.iii. 402)

The last sentence is as revealing as could be, since Leibniz is here considering what is, *prima facie*, just such an 'exception' to the rule; and it demonstrates the fact, which has been increasingly obvious throughout the previous paragraphs, that his theory of volition is totally different from Aristotle's despite the similarities that have been noted. For Aristotle discusses the occurrence of *akrasia* at some length, and seems to take the view that it happens when the agent's desires cease to be controlled by his rational judgment: he acts with appetite, he says, but without choice (EN.1111b). Leibniz, by contrast, in the passage quoted above, asserts that the agent actually *chooses* what he knows to be worse, and in accord with reasons, albeit ones that would not generally be regarded as valid.[4] This shows that Leibniz's theory of volition is not, as Aristotle's was, a purely descriptive account of the processes involved in making a rational decision about a course of action. Rather, it is an explanatory theory, adopted as an *a priori* postulate to account for the fact that the deliberations of a rational monad can result in purposive activity. Apart from the points already noted, this is further indicated by a different use of terms. Aristotle classes acts performed without conscious judgment as 'non-voluntary' (EN.1110b); whereas Leibniz, in common with Descartes and many Scholastic philosophers (*83*, 9), classes them as 'voluntary' simply because they are in accord with the desires of the agent (Gr.384).

Leibniz was no doubt induced to grant this *a priori* status to volition by the principle, fundamental to his philosophy, of Sufficient Reason; or, as he sometimes more aptly calls it, the principle of Determining Reason. 'It is, that nothing ever happens without a cause, or at least a determining reason – that is, something that can provide an *a priori* explanation . . . why it is thus and not otherwise' (G.VI.127). The effects of this principle in the present context are easily seen. Given that action results largely from desire, the faculty of judgment is used to explain why we desire one thing rather than another; the judgment is itself accounted for by the combination of taste and perceptions; and where there is no conscious deliberation, the theory of unconscious influence is employed to preserve the rigour of the scheme. Leibniz thus goes to considerable lengths to ensure that our actions are completely determined; and at Gr.482, in a

---

4. There is an interesting correspondence here with Davidson's analysis of *akrasia* (*54*, 111). He distinguishes between a judgment that is made 'in the light of' all the relevant reasons, and one that is actually 'reasonable' by that standard; and asserts that *akrasia* occurs when the judgment is of the former kind but not of the latter. For though the agent acts with a reason, he does not do so for the right reason.

This is to understand it as a failure in reasoning on the agent's part, and therefore he does not seem to capture the notion of weakness of *will* with the success achieved by Aristotle. But his theory would serve very well within the context of the Leibnizian theory of volition; and there are indeed grounds for thinking that Leibniz had some such theory in mind. In the discussion of virtue at the beginning of Chapter 7, it will be seen that there are close similarities with Davidson's ideas. So Leibniz can probably claim to have room for a notion that is at least akin to Aristotle's *akrasia*, even though not identical with it.

passage strikingly reminiscent of the appendix to the first book of Spinoza's *Ethics*, he claims that it is only because we are unaware of this determinism that we seek, in philosophical theory, to preserve 'the imagined chimera of our independence'.

'Determinism', of course, is a name given to a multitude of different theories. In its crudest form, it involves the view that an action is the inevitable effect of its causes : as, in the physical sciences, it is possible to produce an event by combining the conditions that are known to guarantee its occurrence; so, it is held, an action is produced with equal certainty by a combination of perceptions and desires. Hobbes, for instance, maintained something very like this view, as indeed might be expected from his mechanistic psychology (R.83). It might therefore be thought that Leibniz's theory is substantially different, since it aims merely to ensure that actions can be explained after the event, as it were, and not to predict their occurrence in advance. But such a difference is, in fact, illusory. His adherence to the principle of determining reason ensures his firm denial of the thesis of the 'liberty of indifference', which stated that a free choice occurred only when the alternatives were indistinguishable, and which therefore implied the impossibility of explaining the choice. He writes that 'there is never a state of perfect indifference; one could always give the reason for a choice, if one had clearly observed the hidden ways by which the mind arrived at it' (Gr.386). At G.vi.129 he discusses the ancient paradox of Buridan's ass, and though he denies that there could be two bundles of hay absolutely similar, he is bound to admit that if there were, the wretched animal would indeed not know which way to turn – a conclusion stated more formally at Gr.276.[5] Since

5. His denial of the actual possibility of the situation is likewise founded on the principle of sufficient reason, which entails that 'God has not produced two portions of matter exactly equal and alike', since there would be no reason for putting one in one place and the other in another (G.vii.393). This gives rise to his further principle of the Identity of Indiscernibles which is discussed later.

The consequence that every choice must have a determining reason itself implies that choices cannot always be made for reasons connected with the value of the alternatives. The most striking instance of this occurs at C.376, where Leibniz maintains that if one had to choose one out of four objects, three of which are apparently similar, the only rational thing to do would be to choose the one that is different: since only thus could one give

he thus clearly maintains that when there is no reason, there can be no choice, he must be committed to the belief that every choice is the result of a determining reason; and since there is always such a reason present in every choice-situation, it is an inevitable consequence of his theory, as of that of Hobbes, that 'all occurrences are predetermined' (G.III.168).

Being fully aware of these implications, Leibniz naturally goes to some lengths to show that they present no threat to freewill. At G.VI.288, he writes that liberty consists in the three elements of intelligence, spontaneity, and contingency. The first two of these will be considered here, the third being reserved for the next chapter.

Spontaneity is defined as the freedom from constraint or compulsion (G.VII.109). This would appear, at first sight, to be a purely physical condition, rather like saying that I did not behave freely because I was pushed by someone else. But in fact Leibniz tends to interpret spontaneity in a more metaphysical sense, rather as Aristotle (EN.1110a) and Spinoza (S.I.37) had done, as meaning that the 'source' of the action must lie 'within' the agent himself. The trouble with this notion is, and always has been, that it is extremely difficult to specify just what is to count as an 'internal' source of action. There is a good sense, for instance, in which a man who threatens me with a gun 'compels' me to act as much as one who pushes me; but if fear, and hope similarly, is therefore regarded as 'external', the notion of spontaneity begins to narrow rapidly towards vanishing-point. Difficulties such as these perhaps account for a change in Leibniz's ideas on this topic. In 1689, for instance, he gives qualified assent to the objection that 'the reason of volition comes from external things, namely, from physical temperament and the impression of the object', and consequently defines spontaneity in terms of 'primitive dispositions' (Gr.327). These dispositions

---

a reason for the choice. A comparable example is the case of tossing a coin, mentioned earlier in the chapter. Leibniz maintains (rather plausibly) that we choose one face of the coin for unconscious reasons; but since the choice must be founded on a conscious judgment, we are prone to say that the face is 'lucky', even though the probability of its coming up is equal to that of the other face.

A full discussion of the paradox of Buridan's ass, and of what he calls 'choice without preference', is given by Rescher (*112*).

are totally mysterious, being neither defined nor mentioned elsewhere; they are not the 'taste', at any rate, since that is here
referred to as the 'physical temperament'. No doubt recognising
that this line of argument was going to lead to a dead-end, he
shifted his ground in later years; and claims in 1710 that 'the
representation of outward things' is an essential part of 'the
internal principle of our actions' (E.642). Beyond this, however,
the concept of spontaneity remains undefined and obscure.

In any case, one needs to observe that spontaneity does not
really counter the basic thesis of determinism, since it merely
places a restriction (or is supposed to) upon the kinds of determining reasons that are operative. Leibniz would never deny that
a spontaneous act, like any other event, could be accounted for
in the standard fashion. This point has perhaps been overlooked
by Couturat, who claims that the spirits' actions are free because
they are unpredictable, and not subject to the general laws of
nature (57, 33). It is indeed true that their actions cannot be
forecast by means of the same regularities that appear in the
case of purely physical events; but even their purposive behaviour
is, at least in theory, accounted for by particular perceptions
and desires. A consideration of this point reveals a further fatal
weakness in the concept of spontaneity. Since, according to
Leibniz's metaphysics, every perception and desire arises from
within the monad itself, it should follow that every action, indeed
every event, is really spontaneous; in which case, the notion
must cease to be of any use as a criterion for free actions. This
too arises because the notion is not defined with sufficient clarity.

The criterion of intelligence, however, is more adequate for
its task, since it serves to mitigate the effects of determinism. At
G.III.403, for instance, Leibniz claims that though my present
choice may be determined by the situation in which I find myself,
I can bring myself to choose differently when similar circumstances arise in the future. An analogous capability is found
with physical appetite : I can prevent myself feeling hungry in
the evening by taking a large lunch (E.631). The point is the
same as that made by Broad (in criticism of Spinoza, 47, 28)
who observes that we have 'second-order conative tendencies' :
in other words, we can approve or disapprove of our first-order
value-judgments, and this may have a profound effect upon the
way we finally decide to act. This theory clearly depends upon a

distinction between reflective reasoning and practical judgment, which may be found at E.641 where Leibniz distinguishes the 'judgment of the understanding' from the motives that give rise to action. Accordingly, he is able to account for the important fact that the acquisition of wisdom through experience may substantially alter a man's behavioural dispositions. This reflective consciousness, moreover, can affect not only the way a man chooses, but whether he makes a choice at all; for Leibniz observes that 'the mind is able not only to choose between alternatives, but also to suspend its judgment' (Gr.385). Thus what Scholastic philosophers had called the 'freedom to act', as well as their 'freedom to choose', is incorporated into Leibniz's system by means of intelligence.

Not even intelligent behaviour, of course, can escape from the all-embracing principle of determining reason; and Leibniz is again bound to admit that our most rational choices are determined in their fashion, though the reasons for them may not be apparent to the observer. So, it may be said, intelligence does nothing to free us from determinism. But it should be observed that the determinism with which we are now dealing is very different from the Hobbesian variety considered earlier : it is no longer an automatic, quasi-mechanical process, but a procedure of which the individual is conscious and over which he has at least some control. It is not determinism as such, in fact, that constitutes a threat to freedom, but only a determinism in which the mind of the agent has no part. When made a conscious process of the intellect, it becomes logical deliberation. Thus Leibniz, like Spinoza, claims that 'we are slaves when we are controlled by our passions', but that we become free when our actions are determined by reason (Gr.481).

This observation reveals that intelligent behaviour is not necessarily the norm for the spirits. In fact, in Dewey's words, 'it is the ethical ideal; it is something to be attained; it is action in conformity with reason, or insight into the spiritual nature of reality and into its laws; it is not the starting-point, it is the goal' (52, 339). For Leibniz himself comments that men, who act unreflectively for most of the time, are thus far really very little different from the beasts (G.vi.600). One can therefore see that intelligence is used as a criterion of freedom in two senses. In the minimal sense, it demonstrates that no spirit is wholly controlled by external physical impulses, and therefore escapes the total determination of natural mechanisms. In the maximal sense, it shows that every spirit is ideally capable of acting always in accordance with conscious rational judgment of an end : a usage that makes real the possibility of deliberate voluntary action, which is an obvious necessity for moral theory.

As a criterion of freedom, logical contingency is given far less prominence by Leibniz than either spontaneity or intelligence. Admittedly, it forms the dominant theme of his correspondence with Arnauld in 1686; but thereafter it is mentioned only occasionally, and more often in the context of logic than of ethics. But the critics of his ethical system have made it their main point of attack, maintaining that his account of it is quite inadequate, and that therefore the spirits are bound up in a scheme of rigorous necessitarianism that destroys all hope of freedom. It will be argued in this chapter that such criticisms frequently involve a serious misunderstanding of Leibniz's arguments, fostered, no doubt, by inconsistencies and ambiguities in his own presentation of them.

Contingency is designed to counter the threat to freedom arising from three theories in the realm of metaphysics and logic : namely, the theory of monadic identity, the theory of the creation, and the theory of truth. They can be stated here only in the briefest of terms, and the reader who would understand them further is advised to consult such works as Parkinson's (*103*) or Ishiguro's (*76*) which discuss them in more detail.

The theory of monadic identity, first, can be seen as the logical counterpart of Leibniz's assertion that every event in the history of a monad arises from within itself. For he claims that each event in such a history can be represented by a predicate, attached to the individual as its logical subject; that some of these predicates will be deducible from others in the same collection; and that if one gathers together all the remaining predicates that cannot be deduced in this way – the 'primitive' predicates, as he calls them at G.II.44 – they will constitute what is called the 'complete concept' of the individual in question. Such a concept is 'complete' not only in the sense of entailing every predicate that is true of the individual, but also as making determinate reference to space and time; and in this respect, it is to be contrasted with the generic or unspecific concept of a 'kind' (G.II.39). Leibniz further claims that 'it is the very nature of an individual substance . . . to possess a concept so complete that it contains and implies all the predicates of the subject to which the concept belongs' (G.IV.433). Thus, the complete concept is the defining characteristic of a monadic substance. It is also the basis of the monad's identity, in a purely metaphysical sense; for his principle of the Identity of Indiscernibles states that any two substances must have different concepts. The complete concept, therefore, is made the ground for identifying any particular monad as a distinct substance.

Leibniz's theory of the creation follows naturally from the foregoing. Every complete concept in which there is no logical contradiction between the predicates represents a possible individual – in other words, it identifies a substance which we can consistently imagine as existing. Such possible concepts form a series of 'compossible' sets (again, where there is no logical contradiction between them), each of which is the blueprint for a 'possible world', a group of individuals that could co-exist together. Leibniz seems to believe that each complete concept involves implicit reference to every other concept in such a set, just as the perceptions of a monad 'mirror' all the events that occur in the world. Clearly, there is an infinite number of such compossible sets, just as there is an infinity of possible substances. Now these compossible sets are, as we have seen, formed by the demands of logic alone; and therefore, in a very important sense, they are independent of God. As Leibniz likes to put it, they are merely 'understood' by God, for the divine will plays a part only in choosing one of the worlds to create. In conscious opposition to Descartes (G.III.550), Spinoza and Hobbes (G.IV.283), Leibniz insists that this divine choice is not random : for God, like any ideally rational agent, 'is determined by the very essences of possible things to make his choice among them' (Gr.232). As we might further expect from his theory of volition, the basis of this determination is the degree of perfection possessed by the various alternatives : so God, as the most perfect being, is bound to create the most perfect of the possible worlds. Leibniz sometimes describes an automatically self-maximising 'struggle for existence' among the possibles, but this, as I have argued elsewhere (74), is merely an analogue of the process of divine choice, the individuals' 'desire to exist' representing God's desire to create them.

The theory of truth, finally, appears to underlie his account of monadic identity : for it consists in the view that 'the predicate is contained in the subject' in every true proposition, in the sense that 'a man who completely understood the idea of the subject would also see that the predicate belongs to it' (G.iv. 433). It will be noticed, of course, that this is not intended to serve as a criterion of truth, but rather as a definition of what it is for a statement to be true.[6] The view is sometimes described as one of the 'analyticity' of truth; but that term has such misleading connotations in the present context that it will be better to speak of the 'containment' of the predicate by the subject. For, in the tradition of Kant (K.iii.34), we are accustomed to think of all analytic truths as necessary : whereas Leibniz held that a 'contained' truth could be either necessary or contingent, the difference between them being that only a necessary truth can be *proved*. His notion of proof is of crucial importance. It consists in resolving the various terms of a proposition 'into simpler ideas and truths' (G.vi.612); or, in other words, in substituting

6. According to Couturat (51, 216), Leibniz vacillates between two positions: of holding that all truths are consequences of the principle that 'the predicate is in the subject'; and of holding that only contingent truths are, whereas necessary ones follow from the law of contradiction. Though this may be historically true, it seems a false dichotomy. All truth is a consequence of the 'predicate in subject' principle, for this is an analysis of what it is to *be* true. The reason *why* a proposition is true, however, varies according to whether it is necessary or contingent:

Every truth which is not a statement of identity can be explained. For a necessary truth, this is done by showing that its contrary implies a contradiction; for a contingent one, by showing that there is more reason for its being the case than for the opposite. (Gr.326)

In the latter case, this is the same as showing that the contingent truth follows from the fact that God always chooses the most perfect alternative (Gr.287).

It is also noteworthy that there is a corresponding difference in technical terms. Leibniz's word for 'proof' is *demonstratio*, which cannot be effected in the case of contingent truths (Gr.336). They can only be 'explained' or shown to be true, and this, as in the passage quoted above, is a matter of *probatio*.

logical equivalents for them until the original 'containment' is displayed in the form of an identity-statement (NL.181). If this process is successfully achieved, the original proposition is necessarily true; 'but when you can never reach such fundamentals of the proposition, though you take the analysis as far as you like, you must conclude that it is contingent' (E.641). Thus he maintains that the 'proof' of a contingent truth must involve an infinite number of substitutions (NL.185), rather like an incommensurable number that has definite roots but yet can never be calculated to an exact figure (C.17).

As thus stated, none of these three theories appears to pose any very obvious threat to freedom. However, difficulties do arise when they are combined one with another; and, perhaps more significantly, from the fact that Leibniz himself is unfortunately prone to state them in a misleading fashion, thus inviting some very cogent objections.

A typical instance of this occurs with his handling of the theory of truth. Since the proof of a necessary truth consists in the demonstration of a logical identity, Leibniz often refers to such propositions as ones 'whose contrary implies a contradiction'. If this brief phrase is taken as the sole criterion of necessity, it is easy to involve him in insuperable difficulties. Johnson, for instance, argues from the theory of identity to show that the negation of an individual's act must be self-contradictory (80, 149). To take one of Leibniz's favourite examples, that of the sin committed by Judas Iscariot: it is argued that the predicate 'sinned' must be part of the complete concept of Judas; and that therefore the statement 'Judas did not sin' can be expanded into 'Judas, who sinned, did not sin'. A more evident contradiction it would be hard to find, and therefore we may conclude that his sin was a necessary fact.

It must be admitted that Leibniz makes a number of remarks that invite this kind of argument, not the least of them being his notorious comment in the *Discourse on metaphysics* that Judas had to sin, as 'otherwise he would not be that man' (G.iv. 455). Yet it is difficult to imagine that such an acute logician should have overlooked an obvious weakness like this. Further inspection indeed shows that the foregoing argument is quite invalid. For it commits a *petitio principii*: it assumes that the statement 'Judas sinned' is true, in order to prove that it is necessarily true. And on this basis, it would be easy to construct a purely formal argument that would establish the necessary truth of every proposition. But Leibniz, obviously, does not permit us to make this move. Far from allowing us to assume the truth of the statement, he insists that this is precisely what has to be proved, through analysis of the terms 'Judas' and 'sinned'; the impossibility of achieving this shows that the statement is contingent. His analysis of truth in terms of 'containment' is thus seen to be irrelevant to the question of logical contingency: the crucial issue is his distinction between finite and infinite proof, which, as this example shows, reduces in practice to the criterion that only necessary truths can be shown to be true *a priori*.

It might be said, however, that Leibniz's reply to this objection fails to meet the case. For we know empirically that Judas sinned, and therefore we can be absolutely certain that that predicate is contained in his concept. Moreover, Leibniz tells us that there is a 'law' by which the perceptions and actions of a monad succeed one another, the continuity of which is our ground for saying that the same substance continues to exist (G.II.43,264); and that therefore 'even when Judas was deliberating whether or not to betray Christ, it was already necessary that he would do so' (Gr.270). Hence we may be certain that the instantiation of a complete concept entails all the acts of the individual defined by it: in other words, that the very fact of Judas' existence in this world implies that he will sin. Now this implication is necessary, though it is a purely hypothetical necessity 'which gives no cause for alarm', as Leibniz engagingly puts it at E.630. Yet it shows that the contingency of Judas' sin can be made to depend upon the contingency of his existence, so that if his existence is necessary his acts will be so too. His existence, however, is bound up with that of the world in which he is a member; and accordingly, as Leibniz remarks at G.VII.311, the important question is not whether he will sin, but whether the world that contains him will be chosen above all the others. But we know already, from the theory of creation, that God is bound to choose the most perfect of the possible worlds. Thus the following syllogism can be constructed:

The most perfect world is created by God;
The world that contains Judas is the most perfect;

Hence, the world that contains Judas is created by God.

If we can prove that the premisses are necessarily true (and thus establish the necessity of the conclusion), we shall effectively prove that Judas was not free.

However, this is impossible to achieve. In the first place, the minor premiss cannot be shown to be true *a priori*, since to do so would involve the comparison of Judas' world with an infinite number of others, all of which are infinitely complex. As Leibniz observes :

> Even if a man could comprehend the whole contents of the universe he would still not be able to reveal the reason [for its existence], unless he could compare it with every other possible world. One can thus see why no contingent proposition can be proved, no matter how far the process of logical substitution is carried. (C.19)

We have here an important identification between existential and contingent propositions.

More interesting, at least from an ethical point of view, is the fact that Leibniz wishes to deny the necessity of the major premiss as well. For he writes :

> It is a necessary proposition that 'God wills what is better'. Is it then the case that 'God necessarily wills what is better'? I reply that the word 'necessary' can be applied to the copula itself, but not to what follows it : for God is necessarily a being who wills the best, but not a being who necessarily wills the best. (Gr.494)

Similarly, he claims at Gr.301 that no reason can be given for the fact that God chooses the most perfect world, other than the mere fact that he decides to do so; and, more explicitly, that we cannot prove that God creates what is most perfect 'since the contrary implies no contradiction' (Gr.288). It would seem that Johnson is again wrong in claiming that 'God could not have created any other world than ours without involving *himself* in self-contradiction' (*80*, 150). Where Leibniz does rarely speak of the 'necessity' of God's choice (as at A.ɪɪ.i.117), his remarks refer to the *moral* necessity involved in his theory of duty, which will be explained in a subsequent chapter.

It is therefore apparent that our proposed syllogism must fail to achieve its desired conclusion, since neither of the premisses can be proved to be necessarily true on the basis of the information that Leibniz provides. Rather, he is very careful to point out the contingency involved at every possible point of attack; a concern that sometimes leads to ridiculous straits, as when he suggests a need to prove the identity between this world and the most perfect one (Gr.305). Nevertheless, we can see that contingency is involved at two crucial points : in the entailment of Judas' act by his concept, and in the fact of his existence as a part of the world.

In view of these conclusions, it is possible to dismiss a line of argument that has found favour with a number of commentators, who have tried to show that Judas' sin was not necessary since, in another possible world, there might be an individual in all respects like 'our' Judas except for the fact that he does not sin. In fact, it is only necessary to show that Judas might not have existed at all; but no doubt the inspiration has come from the *Theodicy*, in which Leibniz describes a number of possible individuals whose histories are only slightly different. Abraham, for instance, would assert that the sin is not one of the primitive predicates contained in the complete concept of Judas, for he argues that 'since the connection between the complete concept and derivative properties is contingent, the conjunction of defining predications with the negation of a derivative predication is consistent, and occurs in another world' (*36*, 8). This is indeed possible : at G.ɪɪ.37 (which Abraham cites) Leibniz admits that the primitive predicates in the concept imply the rest only contingently, since the implication depends upon the 'free decrees' of God establishing the fundamental laws of nature. But he goes on to claim that those decrees, combined with the fundamental attributes of an individual, make all his acts certain to occur. Now another possible world would presumably have different laws from this one; and while that would indeed result in the individual behaving differently, it would raise some doubt as to whether our concepts (including the name 'Judas') could properly be applied within it, as Ishiguro has rightly observed

(76, 67). And even if the name 'Judas' could be applied to him, the principle of the Identity of Indiscernibles would imply that he is nevertheless a different individual, so that his possible existence cannot help to establish the freedom of the Judas with whom we are concerned. Although this line of argument thus raises fascinating questions about monadic and personal identity, it is not very promising as a solution to the problem of freedom. Nor is it necessary, since contingency is adequately established by the complete concept itself: as Leibniz says (this time of the sin of St Peter), 'the matter must be proved from the concept of Peter himself – but this is complete, and thus infinite, so that no final proof can ever be achieved' (51, 213).

With the theory of contingency thus explained, it is now possible to discuss its significance as a criterion of freedom. At a very obvious level, it is designed to counter the threat of logical necessitarianism which arises from a number of Leibniz's theories, as we have seen above. With this, its usefulness might seem to be at an end; but Leibniz in fact makes further use of the concept in relation to the threat from determinism. For his theory of volition implies, for instance, that it was absolutely *certain* that Judas would commit the sin he did: but it was not *necessary*, since, to put it crudely, things might have been other than they are. By stressing contingency, therefore, Leibniz is able to emphasise the certainty implicit in his deterministic hypotheses without impugning the existence of freedom. There is always a reason that determines a choice, but it is a reason that merely 'inclines' and does not 'necessitate' (G.VII.110). So it was quite certain that God would choose the most perfect world, but, because there were so many possible worlds from which to choose, his choice was a free one (G.VI.441). And the same liberty is present in the case of human choice, by the mere fact that there is more than one alternative (G.III.472).

Through such considerations as these, Leibniz is led to stress the act of choice as the main practical criterion of free action; for choice can occur only when there are several alternatives, whose very existence guarantees that whatever one decides to do is not the only thing one could have done. This is amply expressed in the following passage, where he employs the analogy of travel to make his point:

When there are many roads available one has the freedom to choose among them, the choice being determined by the fact that one would be better than another. Even when only one road is good, as when there is a bridge across a deep and swift river, one still makes a choice between the bridge and the river – though, of course, the choice is not much in doubt. But if one were in a narrow street between two high walls, there would be only one way to go : and this situation represents necessity. We can see from this that it is not the so-called 'indifference of equilibrium' that constitutes freedom, but the mere fact of being able to choose among a number of alternatives – even though they are not equally feasible or attractive for the agent. (6, 97)

This passage provides an effective summary of the main points in these two chapters. It shows that Leibniz is concerned to emphasise his deterministic theory of volition in order to guarantee that actions can always be explained, and that he realises that this does not inevitably destroy freedom; though, of course, it does mean that his concept of freedom is very different from the idea of 'indifference' that he rejects. It further shows that logical contingency is not, of itself, of great importance : its chief significance lies in focusing our attention upon choice between alternatives as the main criterion of free action. One may conclude that Leibniz has provided himself with an intelligible and workable notion of freedom, overcoming the difficulties that we have seen to arise from his theories.

5 Love and Justice

The previous chapters have dealt with theories that, for the most part, have little ethical content. It has been necessary to consider them at some length since they form the conceptual framework within which Leibniz's system of morality is set; and now we may proceed to examine the fundamentals of that system.

In developing his account of the moral life, Leibniz makes the initial assumption that the moral law often requires us to do good to others, to promote their welfare as an end in itself. This, it should be noted, is not a substantive ethical principle in itself. It is rather a precondition of morality, a definition of altruistic behaviour which any theory of ethics must seek to accommodate. This initial requirement presents Leibniz with a dilemma that forms the crux of his whole ethical system. For his theory of volition, on the one hand, leads to the consequence that all my voluntary behaviour is aimed at the attainment of my own welfare; while morality, on the other, demands that I should act so as to promote the welfare of others. The two theses of egoism and altruism are equally fundamental to his thought, and in sharp conflict with each other. Leibniz, however, was not alone in facing this problem : it was a difficulty encountered by many philosophers who had adopted a similar theory of volition, and they had proposed a variety of possible solutions. Hutcheson, for instance, might be said to have cut the Gordian knot in postulating a large number of different 'motives' such as benevolence, hatred, and self-love (R.315), which was a rather clumsy solution to say the least. Descartes had gone for a simpler answer : he argued that the nature of human society is such that if I do promote the welfare of others, as morality demands, I will myself receive some benefit in the long run (*114*, 95). This is surely a questionable assertion, and cannot properly be accepted without a supporting theory of the political state. A third course had been adopted by Aquinas, who maintained that God is the 'supreme good' that comprehends my own good with that of others; but, apart from the metaphysics involved, this makes all morality a matter of religion.

Leibniz's solution to the problem is more adequate, and more elegant, than any of these alternatives. It hinges upon the logical point that my good, though the formal object of the will, need not be coextensive with its material object; for that may be good for others as well as for myself. Thus he writes:

> There are two ways in which one can desire the welfare of another: the first, that of the scheming man, because it will lead to his own welfare; and the second, the way of the lover, as if it is his own welfare . . . But, you will ask, how can another's good be the same as mine, and even be sought for its own sake? – for it can only be the 'same' in the sense of being a means to my good, not as an end in itself. On the contrary, I reply: it can be an end in itself, it can be sought for its own sake, when it is pleasant. For what is pleasant, and what is sought for its own sake, are identical; and all other things are sought for the sake of what is pleasant, to create it, preserve it, or to remove hindrances from it. (A.vi.i.464)

This argument can easily be understood in the light of the theories discussed in Chapter 2. It was there shown that the good, the 'end' of volition that is sought 'for its own sake', is something that leads to an increase in perfection, and hence gives pleasure to the spirits. If I secure such a good for another, I must accordingly give some pleasure to him – but in doing so, I also achieve some pleasure myself. For the good, *qua* perfection, is a source of pleasure to any rational being associated with it; and furthermore, my act renders the other person more perfect, and his perfection itself functions as a source of pleasure for me. Benefiting another, therefore, also secures 'my own' good, in the sense earlier defined: and thus the requirements of egoism and altruism can both be satisfied. This procedure is what constitutes the Leibnizian concept of 'love'. For he defines it as 'being pleased by the happiness of another; or, in other words, combining another's happiness with one's own' (G.iii.387).

Another point made in Chapter 2 needs to be stressed again here – namely, that Leibniz can solve the problem in this fashion only because of his analysis of value. If the pleasure gained from the possession of an object were itself 'the good', and not the object, it would be impossible for anything to be good for more than one person : and thus the problem would remain insoluble. In this respect, the theory of love seems to have been misunderstood by Matter, who objects to it on the ground that loving another is not being pleased by his happiness so much as by his personal qualities and attributes (95, 301). This very point is in fact implicit in the theory. We are not dealing with the other man's happiness itself, but with the things that make him happy : it is these that are made the objects of volition when we love him. Leibniz's definition of love quoted above may thus be regarded as misleading inasmuch as it obscures this important fact. However, he provides alternative definitions, such as that at Gr.515, in which the issue is made abundantly clear; and it is interesting to note that the basic principle is neatly expressed in Hutcheson's observation that 'the admired quality is conceived as the perfection of the agent, and such a one as is distinct from the pleasure either in the agent or the approver' (R.314).

Although the theory of the good is thus logically prior to that of love, the historical order of their development is the reverse. For Leibniz can be seen to develop his analysis of love in a series of papers entitled *Elements of natural law* (in A.vi.i) during the years 1670–1, at which stage only the rudiments of his theories of goodness and volition can be found in his works. This may well account for the fact that his idea of love differs entirely from those in his usual sources of inspiration. Both Augustine and Aquinas, for instance, regarded love as a general and unspecific tendency towards an apparent good, which finds its counterpart in the Leibnizian system in the concept of *conatus* or desire; whereas Plato, and, to a greater extent, the Italian Platonists such as Ficino and Bruno, had thought of love as an essentially metaphysical striving of spirit which has little in common with human emotions. Nearer to Leibniz's own day, one finds that philosophers such as Hobbes and Spinoza had indeed connected love with pleasure, but had made little reference to the good of others : the latter, for instance, defines it

D

simply as 'happiness attended by the idea of an external cause' (S.i.129, and cf. R.24 for Hobbes). It is only in the works of minor philosophers of that period that one finds any echoes of Leibniz's definition. One of these was John Norris (24, 47), whose book was at least known to Leibniz (G.iii.382); another was Friedrich Spee, whom he mentions with evident approval (Gr.104).[7] Both Spee and Norris, however, thought that love could properly be defined by means of the concepts of 'concupiscent love' and 'benevolent love' developed by Aquinas (ST.iaiiae, 26.4), neither of which accurately represents the notion defined by Leibniz. One must therefore conclude that any similarity between their ideas is mainly verbal, and that his concept of love is both novel and wholly original.

The novelty of his idea is further suggested by the fact that it was a general adherence to the traditional Thomist definitions that led to a widespread controversy about the possibility of disinterested love, which began in 1697. Leibniz immediately saw that his definition would solve the problem, and recommended it as such in his correspondence of that year, relative to the debate in France between Fénelon and Bossuet (D.1.29) and the parallel argument in England between Sherlock and

---

7. Of these two, it is Spee who is generally reckoned to have had the greater influence. Leibniz had met him, and had read his work with close attention, for he praises both the man and the book in a letter to the Princess Sophie of 1700 (G.vii.550). The letter was accompanied by his translation of Spee's dialogue on the three virtues of faith, hope and charity; and it may be found at 5, viii.67–84. The relevant parts of this dialogue, however, are more about the effects of love than its nature, and Leibniz's admiration of it is thus quite compatible with his own different theory. The details of the association between the two men are given by Lieder (88) and Mulvaney (100).

Aquinas' concepts of love referred to in the next sentence are defined as follows:

The activity of love is directed to two objects: to the good which is desired for someone, be it oneself or another; and to the object for which the good is desired. The love of concupiscence is directed towards the good itself, the love of benevolence towards the object for which the good is desired. (ST.iaiiae, 26.4)

Only the latter notion of benevolence figures in the Leibnizian concept of love; the concupiscence for the good itself would probably be akin to Leibnizian desire.

Norris (G.II.569). In both cases, the one party maintained that our love of God could be, and ought to be, free from selfish interest; while the other maintained that this must be impossible, since we never do anything without regard for own interest. As Leibniz observed, his own definition accepted the latter condition, and yet made it possible to love another as an end and not merely as a means (G.III.425).

In classifying a large number of theories of love, Hazo has described Leibniz's as one of 'acquisitive desire', arguing that its essential element is the presence of self-interest which is 'not merely an accompanying and secondary motive but the basic spur from which all love arises' (*68*, 379). This can be accepted only with reservations. Hazo regards Spinoza's definition of love as another of the same type; and though the difference between it and Leibniz's may be largely a matter of emphasis, it is nevertheless sufficiently great to make the classification misleading. This is not to deny the importance of self-interest, for Leibniz himself observes that 'no one deliberately does anything except for the sake of his own welfare; for we seek the good even of those whom we love for the sake of the pleasure we derive from their happiness' (A.VI.i.461). But he insists that we are not necessarily *conscious* of this self-interest, though it may be the 'spur' of deliberate action : for he writes at OH.93 that good things can be desired for their own sakes, 'without any interest in view'. One can therefore reject the criticism made by Kant, who observed that we are indifferent to the fortunes of another except when we happen to be the cause of them (*119*, 66): for this overlooks the all-important fact that good things are pleasant *per se*, no matter what their relation to us.

It will be clear from this that Leibniz's definition of love considerably mitigates the egoistic implications of his theory of volition. His insistence that the will always seeks to achieve the agent's own good does not lead to calculating and exclusively selfish behaviour : its effect is purely negative in practice, since it merely ensures that the agent will not voluntarily do things that he believes to be harmful to himself. Subject to this restriction, the theory of love asserts that one can, and frequently does, seek to benefit other people. It is perhaps worth observing that this is a perfectly valid concept : in the course of our daily lives we often do things to make others happy, and find considerable pleasure not only in doing them but in contemplating the happiness thus produced. It is true that we might prefer to call this 'active benevolence' rather than 'love'; but it is nevertheless a recognisable feature of our emotional lives, and one that has particular significance for the practice of morality.

This observation serves to emphasise an important point about the concept of love – namely, that it is a matter of action rather than sentiment. This will be obvious from its connection with volition, since loving another is merely acting in such a way as to promote the good of another; and because of this, the two elements of the theory of volition are also to be found in the analysis of love. The element of desire, for instance, finds a counterpart in the thesis that we have a natural tendency to love others, which will be discussed in the next chapter. The element of judgment is likewise present, in the guise of wisdom or prudence. This notion combines the ideas of foresight and consideration, since, as Leibniz says in an unpublished piece quoted at *121*, 628, its function is to ensure that what I do for another's good does not turn out to be harmful either to him or to myself. In practice, it is equivalent to the application of the so-called 'golden rule', that one should 'do for another what you would wish for yourself' (M.11): which, as Kant observes, is merely a prudential maxim and not a substantive moral rule (K.iv.430). Leibniz explains this maxim in two ways. First, it is only by imagining myself in the other man's position that I will be able to see all the factors relevant to deciding upon a course of action that involves him (Gr.701). And secondly he argues from the similarity of position at M.70 (as Clarke did also, R.242), to show that whatever reasons I may have for doing something to another will justify him in doing the same to me in a comparable situation.

Given the importance of wisdom, it is only to be expected that its combination with the idea of love will produce a notion of still greater significance. This is the concept of justice, which is the essence of right conduct. It was developed contemporaneously with the concept of love, for its essentials are given in this remark of 1670:

> Since, therefore, justice demands that the good of others be
> sought for its own sake, and since to seek the good of others

in this fashion is to love them, it follows that love is part of
the very nature of justice. And justice will be the habit of
loving others . . . as far as this can be done in accord with
wisdom. (A.vi.i.465)

By the following year, the idea of justice had been formulated
in its final and concise definition as the *caritas sapientis*, the
'charity' or love exercised by the wise man. It is distinguished
from the notion of friendship by the fact that charity is
essentially universal, a benevolence directed towards all men
(OH.95). The 'wise man', of course, is simply the prudent man;
and when his wisdom is linked with love, he becomes a just man
whose acts are always morally right – or, as Leibniz prefers to
call him, a 'good man', a *vir bonus*. Schneiders has argued that
this last concept is merely a cipher, in that Leibniz did not
suppose that any man could be perfectly wise and charitable
(*121*, 620); and in this respect, his theory differs from that of
the Stoic philosophers who believed that one could achieve such
perfection (*71*, 88). His observation is supported by Leibniz's
claim that one does not need to have great knowledge and
intelligence in order to be morally good, since it is sufficient to
model one's conduct on that of the wise man (M.36). But one
should realise that such a paradigm is not entirely hypothetical,
since perfect wisdom and charity are combined in the activity
of God : this is one point at which theology will be seen to be of
vast importance for Leibnizian ethics.

Mulvaney has maintained that this definition of justice was
wholly novel in Western philosophy (*100*), which one might
expect to be the case if the idea of love is as original as has been
claimed previously. Where Leibniz does follow earlier thinkers
is in claiming that justice comprises the whole of right conduct.
Aristotle had thought that justice, in the wider sense of the
term, included all virtuous conduct towards others (EN.1129b);
while Plato, in the *Republic*, had argued that it comprised the
internal virtues of the soul as well. In his early years Leibniz
was concerned to point out his continuity with this tradition,
claiming that justice, like the Aristotelian virtues, can be
regarded as a 'mean' : for he says that it represents a balance
between love and hatred of others (A.vi.i.455). A better way
to put this would be to say that it is a mean between excessive

love for myself and excessive love for others, in which form it was proposed by Butler as the criterion of virtue (*Sermons*, 12.9). In later life, however, Leibniz abandoned this rather unfruitful line of thought, and came to follow Aquinas (*84*) in stressing the importance of wisdom as the common element in all virtue (M.28). By this means, 'right reason' eventually becomes the basic theme of his moral philosophy (Gr.665).

It needs to be noted that the definition of justice is not prescriptive. It does not aim to establish some novel standard of right conduct: for Leibniz in fact believes that this is determined by a set of independent 'moral truths', about which more will be said in the next chapter. All he is claiming is that if we are generally loving and wise, we will behave rightly – it is an analysis of what is involved in being just and morally good. At the same time, the notion of *caritas sapientis* can serve, rather loosely, as a kind of practical maxim. By keeping it in mind we can manage to stay within the bounds of moral rectitude, for we have only to ask ourselves how the good man would act in accord with that principle in a given situation to gain some sort of indication of how we should behave.

In conclusion, it is worth pointing out how the idea of justice is related to the theories previously discussed. We began with the elements of reason and desire, which together form the will. The object of the will was then shown to be anything that increases perfection and thereby produces pleasure: and this makes it possible for actions to be altruistic, while still satisfying the agent's desire for his own welfare. In this way the concept of love is formed, which is finally tempered by prudence to form the idea of justice. The procedure displays a kind of cumulative synthesis, in which possible tensions between reason and emotion, or between egoism and altruism, are progressively resolved. The notion of justice derives great validity from this method of construction.

6   Natural Justice

Given that justice comprehends the whole of moral virtue within its scope, it was almost inevitable that Leibniz would develop the notion further into a complex scheme of related ideas. Fundamental to this process is his distinction between Natural and Universal justice. These, clearly, are not contrary to one another, for the respective opposites would be Legal and Particular justice : Leibniz uses the terms merely to differentiate two spheres within which justice functions. Universal justice carries the implication of perfect benevolence to all men, and consequently refers primarily to the activity of God – it will be discussed fully in Chapter 8. Natural justice, on the other hand, is mainly concerned with the moral conduct of the spirits, and especially of men.

In giving the name 'natural justice' to this use of the concept, Leibniz was deliberately allying himself with the long tradition of jurists who had believed in the existence of 'Natural Law'. It will be remembered that he originally trained to be a lawyer, and that it was during these early years that he wrote many of his most significant works on moral philosophy : it is therefore not surprising that the tenor of his thought is frequently legalistic. The notion of a 'natural law', however, is one that had been understood in a variety of ways by earlier philosophers. Aristotle, for instance, had taken it to comprise the fundamental moral standards and values that are universally agreed upon (EN. 1134b) : this is to think of it as 'natural' in the sense of being a production of nature, something that is naturally the case. Spinoza, by contrast, had conceived it as a 'law of nature' comparable to that of gravity, for example (S.II.189). The main current in this tradition, however, had been that initiated by the Stoic philosophers, who had regarded it as a law discoverable by the 'nature' of man, that is, by his unaided reason (*15*, III.22, & *28*, III.3). It was in this sense that the idea had been further developed by Hugo Grotius, perhaps the greatest jurist of the seventeenth century (*18*, 1.i.10). And Leibniz also followed this line of interpretation. Describing his scheme of justice in a letter of 1671, he remarked that 'it is moreover very practical, since its few basic principles follow entirely from one's reason' (A.ɪɪ.i.109).

The basis of the scheme to which he refers here is a division of justice into three grades or degrees, which are called 'strict justice', 'equity' and 'piety' (A.vɪ.i.343). To these, there correspond three principles or maxims of conduct, which are to harm no one, to give every man what is his, and to live piously. His legal training is again very apparent here since, as he frequently acknowledges, these principles and divisions are the same as the fundamental precepts of Roman Law given at the beginning of Justinian's *Institutes*. To these principles, however, Leibniz attaches three motives of his own invention, which are supposed to induce us to adopt the relative grade of justice; and these will be the main subject of discussion in this chapter. The motives, and their connection with the grades of justice, are displayed in the following table, which is based upon the expositions of the scheme given at M.13 and M.95.

	GRADE OF JUSTICE	PRECEPT	MOTIVE
1.	Personal justice	Harm no man	Self-interest
2.	Social justice	Give each man his own	Sense of humanity
3.	Spiritual justice	Live righteously	Religion

The first motive with which we are concerned is accordingly self-interest or self-regard, by which is meant a purely egoistic concern for one's own welfare. This is to be understood as a consideration for interests which, though self-centred, are nevertheless 'decent and enduring' – in other words, a concern for one's own lasting happiness (Gr.575); for Leibniz will not allow that a brutish search after instant pleasures can lead to right conduct, except by the merest chance. As always, therefore, self-interest is to be subject to prudence. It is this, of course, which explains the fact that self-interest is supposed to induce us to refrain from harming others : for we have seen in the previous chapter that prudence consists in the maxim of doing to others what we would wish for ourselves, and that this is supported by the argument from parallel reasons. So Leibniz is quite justified in claiming that a rational consideration for my own welfare will show me the folly of harming others gratuitously, since, if I do so, they will have a *prima facie* justification for harming me in return.

Inasmuch as self-interest comprises selfish desire tempered by reason, it will be noticed that it is closely similar to the very nature of volition. This is but one instance of Leibniz's general thesis that morality arises from a combination of reason and instinct (A.vi.vi.352); but in the present context, it carries the significant implication that adoption of the first precept is both natural and voluntary, and occurs without the need for any force or compulsion (D.iv.3.273). Indeed, he further asserts at G.vi. 417 that such unconstrained adoption of the precept is essential for virtue. Far from being an arbitrary requirement, this is a consequence of the theory of volition. For the agent has to regard a course of action as being good in order to adopt it voluntarily; and if he does not do so, then, though his act may be morally right, 'he has not the character of being *virtuous*', as Shaftesbury puts it (R.202). It can thus be seen that the first grade of justice, albeit limited in scope and negative in character, is nevertheless a natural and significant beginning to the spirits' moral life.

The 'sense of humanity', the second of the motives in the scheme, is likewise a largely instinctive tendency; and as the first motive corresponds to volition, so this one is related to love (A.vi.i.438). We have seen that love is founded upon the idea of perfection; and when this is coupled with our natural desire for the good in general it yields an inclination to seek the welfare of others, as this comment indicates :

> In fact, our happiness is based upon our natural sensibilities. The more we follow our natures, the more we come to find pleasure in the happiness of others : and it is this that forms the basis of natural benevolence, and of charity and justice besides. (D.v.44)

These words appear in Leibniz's review of the works of Shaftesbury, and are further evidence of his agreement with that philosopher; at the same time, they reveal his disagreement with Hobbes. Writing of the 'natural condition of mankind' in the first book of *Leviathan*, he had argued that our natural self-interest must inevitably lead to 'that condition which is called war', in which the welfare of others is never considered (R.50). Leibniz, however, had seen that self-interest is not necessarily the same as selfishness; and through his theories of love and volition, was able to conclude that it could produce at least a modicum of benevolence without the need for a sovereign authority.

The sense of humanity is supposed to induce the precept of giving to each man what is his (*suum cuique tribuere*). Leibniz gives little indication of what he intends by this principle, which is rather surprising in view of the fact that Plato had demonstrated its disastrous ambiguity (*Republic*, 331). It would certainly be implausible to take it as referring to personal property, what a man owns : since if respect for the possessions of others is to be engendered by a motive, it must surely come from the simple rule of prudence in the first grade of justice. It is more satisfactory to understand it in the sense of what a man deserves, what he should have instead of what he has. This interpretation is supported by a remark at M.95, where Leibniz, in discussing this second motive, says that we are pleased at the happiness of another 'when we see his virtue followed by its deserved rewards'. The precept thus enjoins conduct that goes far beyond that demanded in the first grade of justice : not merely refraining from harming the other man, but actively promoting his happiness when we judge him worthy of it. Equally, it goes beyond the notion of love to something more like justice. There is nothing in the inclination to love that would preclude benevolence towards sinners as well as saints; it is only the element of judgment that brings in the notion of desert, and the distinction between right and wrong.

The third motive in the scheme of natural justice is different in kind from the previous two, being predominantly a matter of intellect rather than of instinct. For 'religion' is intended by Leibniz to mean knowledge of the existence, nature and activity of God. In the present context, God has an essential role to play in ensuring the implementation of the moral law. In conformity with his fundamental premiss of self-interest, Leibniz had written in 1670 that 'I assume . . . that to behave justly without benefiting oneself . . . is the ultimate in stupidity' (A.II.i.30). Since it is an apparent fact that our good deeds are not always beneficial to ourselves, this supposition had to be supported by two metaphysical theses: the immortality of the soul, which allows us a life after this one; and the existence of God, who will reward or punish us in that life in proportion to our virtue or lack of it on earth. These two doctrines were likewise essential for Kant's theory of ethics, though he thought that their truth could only be assumed by the practical reason (K.v.122). But Leibniz, with still unshaken confidence in the powers of *a priori* argument, felt that he could prove them; and significantly claimed to have done so in his earliest extant letter, sent to Thomasius in 1669 (A.II.i.24). The effect of these doctrines in strengthening the principles of justice is expressed as follows:

> If God did not exist, wise men would have no more cause to be benevolent than such as would be required for their own welfare. Nor would they have any reason to seek virtue, other than its intrinsic value, which would be insufficiently strong in this brief life if their souls were not immortal. The existence of God, however, ensures that every good act will be beneficial, and every bad one harmful, to the agent. So that not even a man who endures torture and death for the public good can be regarded as an idiot. (M.21)

As these remarks indicate, the assurance of a just recompense in the next life functions as a motive for right conduct in a variety of ways. Besides ensuring that self-sacrifice is not inherently stupid (a point echoed by Clarke at R.249), it also serves to deter us from doing wrong on occasions when we might be sure of doing so undiscovered (M.55). It likewise dissuades us when we may have a good chance of 'getting away with' our crimes (M.7) – an observation suggesting that divine retribution would be Leibniz's answer to the question posed by Thrasymachus in Plato's *Republic*, of why the all-powerful tyrant should not behave exactly as he pleases, without regard to a moral law.

Yet the fact that eventual retribution is a further motivation towards right conduct is not the only reason for its introduction into the system. As Walker has perceptively remarked, if one believes that virtue is always rewarded it is something of a contradiction to admit the possibility of being a merry sinner or a wretched saint (*129*, 69). Leibniz was aware of this logical conflict, and took steps to guard against it. He argued that God, as the ruler of the kingdom of grace, is concerned to maintain a total harmony and perfection in its operation (A.vi.i.444); and therefore, when a crime is committed, 'the harmony of things demands satisfaction' in the form of punishment (E.643). The two theses of God and immortality are thus well established in his moral philosophy, and serve to reconcile further the principles of benevolence and self-interest.

There are a number of important observations to be made about the whole scheme of natural justice. In the first place, it should be noted that there is a relationship of class-inclusion between its three grades : the sort of conduct involved at the second level includes that of the first, while the 'righteous living' of the third grade comprehends the previous two. An analogous relationship holds between the three motives. Initially, there is merely a consideration of one's own happiness; this is then seen to involve the happiness of others; and finally the awareness of God generates the presence of 'conscience' (M.95), and a steadfast adherence to standards of behaviour. There are no sharp breaks or divisions between these motives : they are stages on a continuous progression of widening consideration that follows naturally, if not inevitably, from the activity of reason and desire. The third grade of justice has the widest scope, and includes not only the social virtues but the more personal ones as well, in the intimate relation between the soul and God. The two previous grades, it should also be said, have a content that is peculiar to Leibniz's system : they do not correspond with the traditional concepts of commutative and distributive justice (57, 54), but rather express a contrast between rational egoism and active benevolence.

It is interesting to note that the three precepts cannot really be taken as criteria by which to judge the morality of particular acts. The first could admittedly fulfil this function to a limited extent, as condemning all harmful acts as wrong; but the third obviously has no direct relevance as a basis for judgment, since it means no more than observing the requirements of morality. The precepts should rather be taken as maxims of conduct; and even more, as Schrecker has contended (*122*, 208), as principles of legislation. For each of them effectively specifies an extent to which the demands of morality are to be observed, and thus indicates a 'grade' of the moral life which the lawgiver can seek to prescribe. Significantly, Leibniz himself states that the purpose of studying natural justice is 'to formulate the laws of an ideal state' (Gr.614). These precepts are therefore similar to the very definition of justice itself, in not being substantive ethical principles; and in 'deducing' them from that definition, Leibniz is merely clarifying its content and not going beyond it to anything new. Friedrich has commented that it is not at all clear what is to be inferred from this deduction, and makes this the basis for his claim that Leibniz has been overrated as a philosopher of law (60). He is right about the lack of implication, but wrong in believing that this represents a failure on Leibniz's part. For, in the only letter he wrote to Hobbes, Leibniz said that he was trying to formulate the basic principle of justice and to derive from it the main principles of Roman Law (G.1.83): in other words, his scheme of natural justice is an end in itself, and is not supposed to imply anything further.

This point is of considerable importance for gaining a correct understanding of his whole philosophy of ethics. As was mentioned in the previous chapter, he believed that the real standards of morality form a system of necessary truths, about which more will be said when we consider his theory of value. Now this premiss has the consequence that one can reason hypothetically, deducing what it would be right to do in a given situation even though it may not actually arise: ethics is thus rather like arithmetic, which does not depend upon the existence of things to be counted (M.24). The idea is further explained as follows:

Jurisprudence is the science of what is just; the science of permissions and obligations; the science of what is right in a given case or act. I call it a 'science' even though it is a practical one, for the reason that all its propositions can be deduced from the single definition of a good man, and do not depend upon induction and examples. (M.85)

This clearly refers to the scheme of natural justice, though it should be realised that Leibniz hoped to push the deduction much farther, to the point of deriving specific laws, and was prevented mainly by a lack of time. This ambition was shared by many other 'natural law' theorists : Grotius, for instance, thought he could prove judicial principles from 'ideas so certain, that no one could deny them' (*18, prolegomena*). But the number of such self-evident moral principles is extremely small, and the majority of those who had attempted such a task had taken as their initial premiss a truth such as 'good is to be done, and evil avoided'. As Nielsen has rightly observed, such a statement is tautologous (*73,* 124). While that certainly makes it self-evident, it also makes it incapable of serving as a premiss from which substantial ethical principles might be deduced : for the only thing deducible *a priori* from a tautology is another tautology. And if further premisses are introduced, such as statements about what is good and evil, the 'deduction from self-evident truths' becomes a sham. Now this is certainly a fair criticism of many works on natural law. But it does not apply to those of Leibniz – since, as we have seen in this chapter, he manages to derive substantial maxims of conduct from his definition of justice with a good deal of plausibility. This fact is of paramount importance. His definition of justice is neither self-evident nor tautologous, and therefore his deductions from it cannot be taken as a quasi-Euclidean 'proof' of morality in the manner attempted by his predecessors. Rather, it is an attempt to *systematise* morality : to reduce it to a few basic principles, and to define its essence in the single notion of justice.

His method can usefully be compared at this point with that adopted by Rawls, who has produced some of the best judicial philosophy in recent years (e.g., *109*). For Rawls can be seen to take the basic notion of a 'just society' as given, and to formulate principles which, if adopted in practice, will realise such a society; an instance is the principle that inequalities between the roles of its members must be generally agreed to be beneficial for all. In precisely the same fashion, Leibniz takes agreed moral standards as his data, and formulates maxims that will yield right conduct in practice. His theory is thus 'meta-ethical' in character, providing a conceptual background to the moral life.

One must finally consider the nature of the link between each motive and its corresponding precept. To some extent, the motive can be understood to provide a psychological impulse; for it is clear that if I do consider my own welfare in a prudent fashion, or if I am mindful of the divine retribution in store for me, it is likely that I will want to behave in the way suggested by Leibniz's maxims. At the same time, however, the motives make it reasonable for me to adopt the precepts. Not only do they give me a reason for doing so : they also ensure that my behaviour will be regarded as sensible by others – for instance, if I am asked why I refrain from harming others, I can provide a justification by pointing out that it is in my own best interests to do so. We have here a further perspective of Leibniz's idea of 'natural justice'. It is 'natural' not only in the sense that its precepts can be discovered by reason, but also in the sense that reason leads us to adopt them.

The third grade of natural justice, which we have seen to include the whole of moral virtue, is represented by the maxim 'live righteously'. The notion of righteousness, however, is not a wholly accurate counterpart for the original Latin term *honestas*, which had played an important part in the ethics of the Roman Stoic philosophers. Cicero, for instance, deals with the idea several times in the course of his *De officiis*: at 1.4.14 he explains that it is linked very closely with the exercise of reason; and at 1.27.94 he comments that 'whatever is fitting or right becomes apparent only when *honestas* is present'. This would suggest a comparison with the metaphorical 'eye' mentioned by Aristotle, which gives us clear 'vision' of right and wrong (EN.1147b). One may say, therefore, that *honestas* is a quality that serves to guarantee correct judgment in ethical matters. It is used in this sense by Leibniz too; the only difference lies in his analysis of this quality, which he takes to consist in the consciousness of God and his retributive function. This gives the notion a theological flavour which it did not have in its original use, and accounts for the fact that Leibniz often uses the term *pietas* (piety) for the same idea.

This being the case, 'righteousness' is merely the antecedent cause and condition of regular virtue, and Leibniz's notion of virtue must be something different. This is indeed so. His idea is foreshadowed by Aquinas' remark that moral virtue 'inclines the desire to the good recommended by reason, which is the right end' (ST.1.aᴵᴵae 58,4), and he defines it as follows: 'virtue is a habit or disposition, which becomes second nature, of acting easily in the manner prescribed by reason; or, more briefly, it is a tendency of volition in the direction of happiness' (M.4). It is interesting to observe the difference between this and Aristotle's definition, which describes virtue as a disposition to choose the right action (EN.1107a). While agreeing with this in thinking of it as a disposition, Leibniz believes that it is not concerned with choosing the act so much as with acting in accordance with the choice: a difference further illustrated by his remark at M.11, that whereas Aristotle held that the right aim of action is to be discovered by virtue, he maintains that it is discerned by charity or love. In other words, his concept of virtue is closely similar to the notion of 'strength of will', as expressed in a further definition of the concept as 'a certain strength of mind, by which we are made to do whatever we believe to be right' (E.72). It should be noted, however, that this does not conflict with the claim made in Chapter 3, that Leibniz's theory of volition leaves no room for the notion of *akrasia* or weakness of will. For when a man acts contrary to what he consciously believes to be the best, Leibniz (unlike Aristotle) can still maintain that he 'willed' to act thus, by appealing to his theory of unconscious motivations; it is only when he consistently acts in accordance with his conscious decision that he can be said to be virtuous. The idea thus bears comparison with Plato's concept of virtue, inasmuch as it pictures a harmonious co-operation between reason and desire (cf. A.II. i.106).

Leibniz was not the only one to make use of such an idea: Spinoza, for instance, likewise speaks of the desire 'by which each man, commanded only by his reason, tries to help others and be friends with them' (S.I.163). He, however, describes this as nobility or magnanimity (*generositas*), and it figures also in the ethics of Descartes (*114*, 85). But Leibniz, rather confusingly, thinks that *generositas* is something quite different. He defines it as the 'consciousness of virtue' (Gr.520): since every good act produces some pleasure for the agent, a lifetime of virtue will give a sustained and refined happiness that cannot be bettered (G.VII.98).

Such happiness, deriving from the exercise of virtue, had been the moral ideal of the Stoics (*28*, IV.2); and Descartes likewise maintained that true happiness was 'a perfect contentment in the soul, an inward satisfaction' (AT.IV.264). Leibniz certainly does not dispute its desirability, and sometimes argues forcefully for the thesis that 'virtue is its own reward' (A.IV.i.530). But he also believes that this would represent the highest good only if

E

there were no life after this one (M.73); and his proof of immortality and God means that his approval of the Stoic ideal can, at best, only be lukewarm (G.vɪɪ.151). He also makes the perceptive criticism that Aristotle's theory of ethics cannot accommodate the level of absolute virtue that is the ideal of Christianity, since, without the premiss of immortality, 'it is bound to concentrate overmuch upon this life' (G.vɪɪ.149). Despite a number of intriguing similarities, therefore, Leibniz's view of the moral life is very different from that of the Stoics and Aristotle, not least in the fact that he conceives true happiness to be a matter of outgoing charitable activity.

The account of virtue and its related notions is further extended by the theory of 'moral qualities'. This, it must be confessed, is one of the more obscure parts in Leibniz's ethical system; but it deserves close attention since it contains his analysis of duty, as we shall see in due course. There are two moral qualities, namely 'right' and 'obligation' – 'qualities', of course, in the sense that an agent can possess them. It is possible that the ideas may have been borrowed from Grotius (*18*, 1.i.4); though Grua suggests that they derive initially from the works of Suarez and his fellow Jesuits, who were the first to use the terms in other than a purely legal context (*65*, 224), a suggestion possibly strengthened by the curious fact that Leibniz deals with the theory only in his Latin works. Certainly, he follows the Jesuits in applying the qualities to purely moral situations. For the basis of his theory is the assertion that the moral worth of an action, whether it is right or wrong, is dependent upon whether the agent had, or did not have, a right or obligation to do it (A.vɪ.i.301).

The two moral qualities are contrary to one another. The possession of a right gives the agent the freedom or 'power' to choose between acting and not acting; an obligation, on the other hand, connotes the lack of such freedom, since the agent is bound to act whether he wants to or not (Gr.706). Because of this, Leibniz describes an obligation as a 'moral necessity' which therefore relates to a 'moral impossibility' : for just as an act is morally possible if one has a right to do it, so it is morally necessary if one is obliged to do so; and the failure to do it is made morally impossible, in the sense that such failure *cannot* be right or correct.[8] It is from this idea of obligation that the analysis of duty will eventually be derived; and it may well have been in Kant's mind when he wrote, in the *Prize Essay*, that an 'ought' expresses 'a necessity of action' (*119*, 24). For the moral necessity clearly represents an obligation to do something, not a 'legal' obligation to someone else. This is a significant point, for it will be seen in the next chapter that God was bound by a moral necessity to create this world, and it would be absurd to interpret this as somehow 'owed' to the beings he created.

The connection between the moral qualities can be further clarified by comparing them with the ideas of other philosophers. Hobbes, as Raphael has observed (*108*), first made the important distinction between 'rights of action' and 'rights of recipience'. In modern jurisprudence, these concepts have been termed 'privilege' and 'right' by Hohfeld (*72*, 36), who observes further that their respective 'jural opposites' are 'duty' and 'no-right' (which is a simple absence of right, the lack of a claim upon another). It is clearly the opposition of privilege to duty that is represented by Leibniz's analysis of obligation as the negation of a right, which demonstrates that he is concerned with rights of action, not of recipience. The fact that he regards the moral qualities as contraries leads him to assert that 'an obligation, which is opposed to a right, involves a limitation upon the agent's freedom and ability to act' (Gr.618); in which it is

8. The originality of Leibniz's ideas on this topic is further revealed by comparing his notion of moral impossibility with that defined by Chauvin (*50*), as 'that without which an effect never or seldom occurs, even though it could theoretically occur'. This is to take 'moral', not in the sense of being concerned with right and wrong, but in the sense of relating to conduct generally: his idea is that of what is 'usually' or 'in practice' necessary for something to be the case.

In this sense, the phrase has passed into English. Relating the consequence of a charitable distribution of Bibles to the poor, Dickens writes '. . . there was such a dropping of books, and rustling of leaves, that it was morally impossible to hear one word of the service for five minutes afterwards' (in *Sketches by Boz*: 'Our Parish – The Ladies' Societies'). We also speak of things being 'virtually' or 'practically' impossible in the same sense.

The concept defined by Chauvin that does come closest to Leibniz's idea is that of 'ethical impossibility', which is 'what is repugnant to right reason, what it is illegal to do, what an upright man finds distasteful'. But here there is not the same association with a practical constraint upon a man's behaviour.

possible that he was consciously echoing the more concise observation made by Hobbes, that 'where liberty ends, obligation begins' (*De cive*, II.10). This opposition has the significant consequence that there are only two alternatives open to the agent : either he is free to act if he chooses, or he is not free and is bound by an obligation. The moral order is thus effectively 'closed', since every act must be right or wrong. The picture this presents is rather like that mentioned by Aristotle, in which the law is assumed to forbid whatever it does not expressly permit (EN.1138a). Grua is no doubt correct in suggesting that this can be seen as a result of the principle of Sufficient Reason, which precludes all 'indifference' in ethics as in other areas of Leibniz's philosophy (65, 230).

It was mentioned above that the moral value of an act is dependent upon the moral qualities of the agent. In fact, however, there is a perfect correlation between the agent and the act; so it can equally be said that the agent's qualities themselves derive from the act. If, for instance, the action which he contemplates is good, then, *ceteris paribus*, he will have a moral right to do it; whereas if the act is wrong he will lack such a right, and consequently be obliged to abstain from doing it. From this it can be seen that the moral qualities are imposed on the agent by the force of logic. As Leibniz says, an obligation 'is laid especially upon the agent who wishes to be called a "good" man' (Gr.607): his obligations constitute the logical criteria for the application of that description to him, since he cannot neglect them and still validly be called 'good'. As Riley has expressed it, 'moral necessity is absolute in the sense that one cannot choose the lesser good and still be right' (*113*, 9). One can therefore see that to every act, right or wrong, there corresponds a moral quality on the part of the agent who intends to do it, which further illustrates the determinate character of the Leibnizian moral order.

This logical analysis of obligation comes to function as a theory of duty through Leibniz's belief that, in the case of the good man, 'what are moral qualities come to be transmuted into natural ones' (M.3). He likewise comments that 'by the word "moral", I understand that which has equal force to "natural" in the case of the good man' (G.III.386). And in support of this statement, as frequently elsewhere, he quotes a remark of the Roman jurist Papinian which runs: 'it is not to be believed that we are able to do things that are morally wrong.'[9]

The meaning of these strange assertions becomes clear when one considers the theory of volition. The good man, it will be remembered, is one whose benevolence is properly under the control of wisdom, and whose judgments are therefore generally correct. This implies that 'the strength of his volition or his inclination towards an object will be exactly proportionate to the degree of goodness in the object' (Gr.468); that is, the degree to which the object is pleasant. Therefore, if the object in question is a wrong act, one that will bring misery in its wake, the moral impossibility of doing it becomes a 'natural' impossibility: not, of course, in the sense that the good man is physically incapable of performing the action, but in the sense that he cannot voluntarily bring himself to do so. Thus Leibniz further comments that the 'moral' comes to have the same force as the 'natural' through 'prudence, right reason, and a concern for one's own welfare' (Gr.721). The basic idea is engagingly expressed in Whichcote's aphorism, that 'what is *Morally* filthy should be Equivalent to what is *Naturally* Impossible: we *should not*, is morally we *can not*' (*106*, 330).

The argument from volition is reinforced by considerations of

9. Leibniz quotes this comment in the words in which it is expressed by Justinian (*22*, *Digest* 28.vii.15), who is himself relating an observation in the sixteenth book of Papinian's *Quaestiones*.

I am grateful to Professor P. G. Stein for explaining the original meaning of the remark. A Roman *paterfamilias* who was unwilling to provide an inheritance for one of his sons had to circumvent the legal requirement to do so; and since an explicit clause of disinheritance would render the will invalid (in which case every son would share in the property), the practice grew up of making such a legacy subject to the fulfilment of given conditions. In such cases, the jurists would consider whether the specified conditions could be fulfilled; and if so, and if the son did not do what was specified, he was deemed to forfeit his inheritance. However, conditions which were contrary to the standards of right conduct (e.g., which involved dishonesty or criminal behaviour) were regarded as being impossible for the son to fulfil, even though he would be physically capable of doing them. (In such a case, he would be given a share according to the procedure for invalid testaments.)

It is not clear whether Leibniz was aware that Papinian's comment concerned only such specific cases; though he should have learnt this while studying the law. He definitely goes beyond the scope of the original in making it a universal maxim of ethics.

religion, since the retributive activity of God helps to ensure the coincidence of self-interest and morality:

> Since a right is a power, and an obligation a necessity, imposed upon the man who wishes to be just, it will have force also for the man who wants to be 'saved'. The wise man already knows, and the fool will learn by his misfortune, that the prudent man cannot do things which conflict with piety, justice and honesty, things which are morally wrong and ought not to be done; and, by contrast, that it is to everyone's greatest benefit to seek virtue and praise, and to develop righteousness above all. (M.3)

A similar argument lies at the root of Molina's treatment of the moral qualities, which Schiedermair has suggested was the model for Leibniz's theory (*118*, 75). To sum up, then, it can be seen that the Leibnizian analysis of duty depends upon the thought that when a good man knows that he ought to behave in a certain way, because that act is right, he will understand that obligation as limiting his moral freedom; and since he is concerned always to be morally right, that will come to limit his practical freedom as well, in the sense that he will not feel himself to be free to act in any other way.

This is the theory which Kant's analysis of duty was later to supersede; and as such, it is interesting to examine Kant's implicit criticisms of it. The chief of them, from which others follow, is that it is 'heteronomous' in Kantian terminology (K.IV.441) – that is to say, the force of duty is dependent upon 'the agent's willingness to engage in the relevant activity or practice', as Black explains it (75, 111). This is evident from the arguments considered above, both of which draw their force from the theory of volition, especially from the element of self-interest. Even though the moral 'rightness' of an act is determined independently of the agent, his feeling that he must do it derives from his desire for the pleasure that the performance will involve, or for the reward that will eventually be given him by God. And further criticisms follow from this. For one, the force of Leibnizian obligation is dependent upon a subjective and contingent condition (i.e., that the agent wants to be happy, and realises that moral virtue is the only means to this end), and therefore it cannot be the 'absolute' necessity which true duty is (K.iv.416): though the agent *is* obliged to act (logically), he does not necessarily *feel* himself to be. The same point is made by Von Wright concerning what he calls 'technical norms', whose very existence is conditional (*127,170*). In Leibniz's theory, if the agent fails to recognise the desirability of a virtuous life, 'moral necessities' have no claim even to be considered by him. A further criticism made by Kant is that, according to Leibniz, the end which the agent is obliged to seek is 'not something good in itself, but a state of well-being: not a concept of the reason, but an empirical idea of a certain state of feeling' (K.v.62). Whence he argues that Leibnizian duty, unlike his own, cannot arise from the supreme authority of pure reason alone.

Without attempting to deny the truth of these observations, it must be said that Kant more than once betrays some misunderstanding of Leibniz's philosophy. At K.v.26, for instance, he claims that it could be only a contingent fact that men's desires are directed to the same end. Leibniz would admit that things might be different in another possible world, as we have seen in Chapter 4; but with matters as they are he would deny Kant's claim, since his emphasis on desire as the very essence of mind and its necessary attraction towards perfection indicate a fundamental coincidence of ambitions. Again, Kant himself admits that an agent whose will is controlled by his reason 'conceives as subjective necessities . . . whatever he discovers to be objectively necessary' (K.iv.412). This is already implicit in Leibniz's thesis that desire is consequent upon judgment; and though Kant intended that the influence of desire upon reason should be removed, this presents as much difficulty in his account as it does in that of Leibniz.

The real ground for disagreement between the two philosophers lies ultimately in the fact that they have different conceptions of duty, and wish it to serve a different purpose. Kant, for instance, eventually tries to derive the standards of moral good and evil from the notion of duty, whereas Leibniz attempts to explain duty in the light of standards already given. The difference is particularly obvious in the relationship between duty and desire. Since Kant holds that duty should come from reason alone he regards them as fundamentally opposed, and therefore concludes that an action has real moral value only when it is done from a sense of duty that runs counter to the agent's inclinations (K.iv.398). Leibniz, on the other hand, thinks that moral perfection involves the coincidence of duty and desire, and this is precisely what he tries to express in relating 'moral' and 'natural' necessity so closely to one another. While he might therefore agree with Kant in thinking that benevolent inclinations, or 'pathological love', cannot be commanded, he would disagree with the conclusion that it therefore lacks moral worth (K.iv.399); for the third grade of justice that we have been considering involves exactly this kind of natural benevolence.

It must be concluded, however, that Leibniz's theory of duty is really rather inadequate. Not that it is philosophically incoherent, for it is intelligible in itself and is consistent with his other theories; but from a practical point of view, it is implausible to suggest that the desire for happiness could make it impossible for the good man to behave wrongly as it is supposed to do. It is tempting, and perhaps not wholly incorrect, to attribute this failure to the traditional ideas with which Leibniz was working. Earlier philosophy had been dominated by the Greek notion of duty, succinctly described by Maritain as that of 'a masterful ordering of means' (94, 34): it had been thought that one ought to behave rightly in order to achieve eventual happiness. This is markedly different from the Judaeo-Christian notion, according to which one is under an absolute command to behave rightly, simply because this is good. Leibniz can be seen as striving to accommodate this latter notion within the conceptual framework that had been developed to deal with the former, for this explains his repeated emphasis upon the 'necessity' of obligation and its real constraint upon conduct. He manages to produce a theory of duty that is far stronger in effect than anything proposed by Plato or Aristotle, but ultimately he fails in his appointed task. It was achieved in the end by Kant, but then only by developing a new scheme of concepts and a novel approach to moral philosophy.

8   The Best of all Possible Worlds

Since the time of Voltaire's entertaining lampoon in *Candide*, Leibniz has been notorious as the man who thought that this is the best of all possible worlds. Philosophers have recognised that this assertion relates to several metaphysical theories of fundamental importance; but it is not so widely realised to be a thesis of considerable moral significance as well.

Such ethical significance derives not only from the characteristics of the world, but also from the very process of its creation, which has been sketched briefly at the beginning of Chapter 4. It was there stressed that God's choice is wholly determined by the uncreated concepts of possible worlds. Those who believe with Russell (*115*, 3) that Leibniz's philosophical speculations were limited by 'the fear of admitting consequences shocking to the prevailing opinions' should notice that this fundamental thesis is clear evidence to the contrary : for it contradicts the theories of most Scholastic thinkers (*78*, 206) and of Descartes (AT.vii.431); and had been authoritatively condemned by St Augustine as 'sacrilegious' (*12*, *Div. quaest.* 83, 46). The only near precedents to be found, indeed, are Plato's account of the creation (*Timaeus*, 29), and the later version of the same as developed by the Cambridge Platonists in opposition to Calvinist thinking (*49*). The significance of Leibniz's disagreement with the current orthodoxy on this point lies in the fact that it was motivated by a desire to ensure the moral goodness of God. For he realised that in the absence of any criteria determining the divine will, there could be no real assurance that God's acts are truly good – 'for why should we expect good things from him rather than bad ones, if his choice is made by a blind desire devoid of reason, i.e., by a mere wish?', as he demands at A.ii.i.299. He therefore makes a distinction between two aspects of the divine choice, pointing out that the mere act of will can only account for the fact that a

world exists, whereas the wisdom behind the act, exemplified
in the reasons for the choice, explains the fact that it is this
world rather than another which was created (NL.171). As he
notes at BH.58, God's choice of this world thus comes to serve
as a substantive ground for the principle of sufficient reason,
since it explains why things are as they are and not otherwise.

Yet its degree of perfection could not account for the existence
of the world were it not for the further premiss, that God
desires to create the most perfect of the possible worlds; and this
is a consequence of God's own perfection, whence arises the
moral significance of the creation-process. As the most perfect
being, the *ens perfectissimum*, God displays both perfect benevolence and perfect wisdom in all his activity (G.VI.107), whence
it follows that his acts are perfectly just since these are the two
constituents of justice. Mulvaney has argued convincingly
(87) that Leibniz can be seen to explain this fact at the beginning of the *Discourse on metaphysics* : having established the
perfection of God's nature, he asserts (in sections 3–5) that he
obeys the moral law, or 'lives righteously', that he causes no
injury in the act of creation, and that he gives to each monad
what is its 'due'. The three precepts of justice are thus evidenced
in the process of creation, and display the moral as well as the
metaphysical perfection of God. From this, there follows the
important consequence that God is an instantiation of the concept
of a 'good man', as mentioned in Chapter 5; and that the
principles of justice are not mere theoretical ideals, but are
clearly exemplified in divine activity.

The unrestrained and perfect benevolence of God leads
Leibniz to describe his activity as 'universal justice'. While the
scheme of natural justice is mainly concerned with the motives
that make it reasonable to behave rightly, the notion of universal
justice deals more with the practical implementation of the
precepts, with the aim of 'arranging everything for the greater
good of all' (M.14). However, the notion of justice itself under-
goes no alteration, since the same three precepts and the basic
definition remain unchanged. Leibniz maintains that the aim of
universal welfare is manifest in God's government of the spirits
in the Kingdom of Grace (Gr.608).

Although the precepts of justice are implemented in the
creation, it must be stressed that this is so only because God

obeys them : for the laws of justice themselves are 'anterior' to the creation, if such a word may be used of a situation in which time does not exist. As Leibniz expresses it at Gr.252, 'the ultimate rule of justice is not the will, but the wisdom of God' – meaning by this that God 'understands' the principles of justice in the same way as he conceives the ideas of the possible worlds. This is so because those principles are 'eternal' (E.634): i.e., they are necessary truths, dependent upon a conceptual 'proportion', and not upon actual cases (M.24). God can nevertheless be regarded as their source :

> What is true remains true even though it may not be known by any man; and what is good retains its goodness, even though no man makes it his standard. If there were no God, however, nothing would be actual or indeed even possible, and thus both truth and goodness would not exist. One may therefore say that Truth can be identified with the understanding, and Goodness with the will, of the First Cause – which is God. (Gu.ii.35)

God is therefore conceived as both immanent and transcendent in the context of morality : immanent, in the sense that his acts are subject to the rules of justice, and transcendent in the sense that they could not be instantiated without him. Politella has perceptively remarked that such a relationship between immanence and transcendence is 'fundamental to every system striving for logical consistency' (*107*, 24).

Yet how are the principles of justice 'necessary', and why is God bound to obey them? The answer to this comes from the remark noted in Chapter 6, that the precepts can be deduced from the very definition of a 'good man'. This implies that the precepts will be binding upon any being capable of love and wisdom; that is, upon any 'person', defined by Leibniz as a being that can possess moral qualities through its having both reason and will (M.107). Since God obviously possesses both attributes, he is the 'author' of justice 'by his very essence, not by his will' (D.iv.3.273) – in other words, the divine nature itself makes God subject to the moral law. This yields a further sense in which justice can aptly be described as 'universal', namely, that it applies to every intelligent monad in the universe, not merely to

mankind alone (D.IV.3.261). And the aim of justice, of promoting the common good, applies not merely to human social
welfare but to 'the perfection of the universe and the glory of
God' (Gr.638).

It is interesting to note that Grotius had sought to establish
a scheme of natural justice on the basis of the needs of human
society alone, and had therefore observed that it would retain
its validity even if God did not exist (*18, Prol.*11). Leibniz
remarks upon this observation, in an early paper (A.VI.i.431),
that it would still be desirable for men to believe in the existence
of God for the sake of the consequent psychological inducement
to behave rightly; but he none the less recognised the truth
in Grotius' comment, for he writes in 1701 that 'it is not a
necessary requirement for the formal basis of justice that it
should be a rule promulgated by a higher authority' (Gr.665).
He is here explicitly denying Aquinas' definition of law (ST.
IaIIae, 90.4), and further stating the autonomy of justice
according to his own system.

The fact that God, like any other spirit, is thus necessarily
subject to the demands of justice means that he ought to behave
in the best way; it is his duty to do so, and he is constrained by
the moral necessity of this obligation. In the present context,
this implies that God is bound to create the best of all possible
worlds, whence one may draw the important conclusion that it
is absolutely certain that he will choose the best – even though,
as we have previously seen, it is a contingent fact that he does so :

> And thus we have a physical necessity derived from meta-
> physics. For though the world is not metaphysically neces-
> sary, in the sense that the contrary would imply a contra-
> diction or logical absurdity, it is nevertheless physically
> necessary, or determined in such a way that the contrary
> would imply an imperfection or moral absurdity. (G.VII.
> 304).

One should not be misled, as Russell (*115*, 122) and Rescher
(*111*, 28) appear to have been, into thinking that the phrase
'imperfection or moral absurdity' somehow implies that perfection is *per se* morally good. If some other world had been
chosen instead of the most perfect, the implication would be that

God had failed to fulfil his duty (and is thus less than perfect), and his act would be a 'moral absurdity' or impossibility, a denial of the moral necessity of his obligation.

Now the fact that the creation is portrayed as a matter of choice, made in conformity with the moral law, means that the world must be a 'good' thing in Leibniz's usual sense of that term. For the world is an object of volition, and all such objects must be regarded as good, as we know. This is why Leibniz speaks of the 'best' of all possible worlds; and we shall now examine what that epithet means in this context, since few others have troubled to do so. The majority of commentators have concentrated on the doctrine that this is the 'most perfect' world: perhaps understandably, since its fruitfulness is indicated by Beck's list of no less than eight important metaphysical theories that derive from it (42, 227). But Leibniz asserts that the world is morally good as well as metaphysically perfect (G.vi. 242), and this is at least as important from his point of view. Of course, its goodness is a consequence of its perfection, and this has led Rescher to argue that perfection is ultimately the more important criterion (112, 166); citing as evidence a passage from the *Theodicy* in which Leibniz suggests that perfection might outweigh moral evil (G.vi.378). But the tone of that passage is very tentative, and strong conclusions should therefore not be drawn from it.

To demonstrate that Leibniz can justifiably argue that the world is 'good', one must inevitably begin with its degree of perfection, since goodness is analysed in terms of the pleasure resulting from increased perfection. The world's perfection, however, is itself a partial result of the process of creation, especially when this is seen as 'a conflict for existence' that automatically produces the largest compossible set of possible individuals (74).[10]

10. Though perfection is thus the reason for the existence of things, one must not be misled into thinking that existence itself thereby adds to perfection, as this would produce a circular argument. Leibniz analyses existence in the same way as Berkeley, on the basis that 'to be is to be perceived' (Gr.267). He discusses its relation with perfection as follows:

We tend to think of existence as having nothing to do with the essences [i.e., concepts] of things. But this cannot be: there ought to be more in the conception of something as existing than as not existing, which would make existence a perfection. But in fact existence

This multiplicity of different individuals is what Leibniz calls 'variety'. However, he also stresses the criterion of 'order' believing (quite plausibly) that it is only in an ordered series that maximal variety can be achieved, since a random series might well leave 'gaps' into which further possible individuals could be fitted. The perfection of a complex system such as the universe is thus to be understood as a function of variety and order together (GW.172). The combination of these produces the single Leibnizian concept of 'harmony', which is found 'when many things are summoned together into a kind of unity' (Gr. 12). Obviously, however, the two criteria are in partial opposition, for the most 'unified' world would be one in which there existed only a single substance; and it is therefore possible that, as Leibniz maintains, there is only one point at which the criteria can be maximised, representing the single most harmonious universe. The notion of 'the most perfect world' at least has a specifiable content, a point missed by Ahern who falsely supposes that variety is the only criterion and thus concludes that it is as meaningless as 'the longest possible line' (37, 62). Furthermore, the notion has strongly aesthetic connotations. Leibniz frequently comments that harmony involves proportion, regularity, or 'form', and thereby implies that the fundamental organisation of the universe is not without a certain beauty and attractiveness of its own.

This notion of metaphysical harmony is not to be confused

---

can only be explained as membership of the most perfect series of things. In the same way we understand the notion of position: it is an extrinsic quality that adds nothing to the thing given in itself, but it adds the means whereby it can be affected by other things. (C.9)

The relation between perfection and essence is explained further in Chapter 11. For the present, this passage simply means that existence is a second-order or 'extrinsic' quality: that a certain concept figures in the greatest compossible set is not a further predicate *within* the concept itself, but a predicate *about* the concept as a whole. It therefore adds nothing to the concept, but it does add to our conception of the object which the concept represents.

Leibniz can be seen to develop this view of existence as a second-order predicate during his early correspondence with Eckhard (G.1.209 ff.). The clearest statement of his final view is to be found in a longish passage at BH.119.

with that of the pre-established harmony, the thesis that the perceptions of a given monad correspond with those of all the others. Yet this thesis is rightly called 'harmony' inasmuch as it guarantees that a fundamental order and regularity underlies the multifarious experiences of an infinity of substances. The practical effect of this is that the perfection of the world is correlated with a maximal degree of 'positive comprehensibility' (GW.161), by which Leibniz means that general 'laws of nature' may be formulated which enable us to understand the observed succession of events (ibid.170). The pre-established harmony further implies that the spirits are inevitably bound together in a single community, since the welfare of one must have repercussions upon the welfare of all. Plato had stressed the importance of presenting such an idea of society in moral education (*Laws*, 903b), and Leibniz likewise develops its ethical implications. He shows how it reinforces the possibility of altruism by ensuring a real identity between one's own good and the good of others (M.31); and, employing an arithmetical analogy, he comments that benevolence has 'the form of multiplication, not addition' (A.II.i.174), by which he means that the good I do to another adds not only to his pleasure, but to the pleasure of all the spirits. This is one instance of his general claim that the operations of the Realm of Nature, the basic metaphysical processes, serve the interests of the superior Realm of Grace (G.IV.479): for, implying as they do that every act has infinite consequences, they stress the seriousness and universality of the principles of justice. Leibniz also develops the same general notion in a theological perspective. He points out that the spirits' perception of the universe is 'like an echo, a reflection or duplication, of its harmony', which constitutes the reason for God's creation of rational beings (A.VI.i.438): for this 'reflection' is the same thing as praise or glory, and 'God made the creatures, especially those with minds, for the sake of his glory' (G.VII.74). This view bears close comparison with Aquinas' belief that the fact of creation is accounted for by the tendency of divine goodness to 'diffuse' itself (*63*, 102), though one should also note Leibniz's assertion that this world was chosen because it contained the person of Christ (G.VI.446).

The concept of harmony, in both its perspectives, is therefore relevant to the issue of moral goodness insofar as it accounts for several important aspects of the Kingdom of Grace. But it also serves as a premiss which straightforwardly implies that the world is good. Leibniz appears to have two distinct arguments for this, the first of which uses the word 'good' in the simple sense of 'pleasant'. Maintaining as he does that God seeks to achieve the greatest general good in accordance with universal justice, Leibniz must think, with Cumberland (R.107), that the creation produces a maximum of happiness for all. And this comes about because the spirits' perception of the perfection of the universe, which is the greatest possible, gives them a maximum of pleasure from contemplating it :

> And thus it follows that the world is a whole, filled with embellishments, and thus designed to give the greatest pleasure to a rational being; for such pleasure is simply the perception of beauty, order and perfection . . . Its first cause is one of supreme *goodness*. For when a maximum of perfection is produced in reality, a maximum of pleasure is afforded to our minds. (G.VII.290)

Leibniz develops this theme at some length in his work *On happiness*, where he rhapsodises about the beauty of nature, the 'sympathy' we feel with it, and the 'sweetness' of contemplating its glories (E.671). His first argument, therefore, combines the premiss of harmony with the premiss that 'pleasure is the perception of harmony' (A.VI.i.484), to conclude that it is a pleasant place for the spirits who inhabit it – and this is to conclude that it is 'good', in Leibniz's sense of that term.

His second argument is more explicitly concerned with the Kingdom of Grace, and depends upon the premiss of God's retribution after death. For it is this just retribution which ensures that 'all moral goodness becomes physical . . . or that every good act is pleasant' (A.VI.vi.250); or, as he puts it at Gr.393, that 'moral perfection is the physical perfection of rational beings'. When he talks of 'physical perfection' or 'physical good' in these contexts, Leibniz is not meaning that moral virtue is somehow 'natural' or 'essential' with regard to the spirits, as Schrecker has mistakenly contended (*123*, 505). He is simply referring to his theory, already mentioned in Chapter 2, that there are three kinds of 'perfection' that can be regarded as good : moral, which is virtue; physical, which is pleasure; and metaphysical, which will be considered in Chapter 11 (G.iii.32). In other words, his basic argument is that moral virtue proves to be pleasurable for the spirits. This is presented as follows :

> You must not deny the existence of moral perfection, or goodness, because of a supposed confusion at this point between it and metaphysical perfection, or magnitude. You must realise that my argument implies two things : not only that the world is physically the most perfect, or metaphysically if you prefer, in the sense that it is the set of substances containing the maximum reality; but also that it is the most perfect morally since, in fact, moral perfection is physical so far as minds are concerned. The world is not just an especially wonderful mechanism : inasmuch as it is composed of minds it is also the best political state. For it bestows upon those minds a maximum of happiness and joy, which is their physical perfection. (G.vii.306)

In this second argument, then, the physical pleasure of the spirits ensues not upon their contemplation of the world, but upon their activity in accordance with the principles of justice, for this is not only intrinsically pleasant but also duly rewarded by God. The basic thesis is admirably expressed in Butler's contention that 'duty and interest are perfectly coincident . . . this being implied in the notion of a good and perfect administration of things' (R.409).

When Leibniz asserts that this is the best of all possible worlds, it can thus be seen that he does so consistently with his own premisses. For him, something is 'good' if it produces pleasure as a result of its degree of perfection : consequently, this world is the 'best' because it is the most perfect of possible worlds, and therefore produces a maximum of pleasure for the spirits (who are, of course, the only beings able to experience it). The arguments outlined above are complementary : they both show how the organisation and operation of the universe function as such a source of pleasure, but the first deals mainly with the Realm of Nature, while the second concentrates upon the Realm of Grace. From the standpoint of ethical theory, the

F

latter is undoubtedly more important. The Realm of Grace is, after all, the sphere within which morality operates, and its presence in the created order of things is a factor of great significance. For, as the general argument of this chapter has shown, God's subservience to the demands of universal justice guarantees the existence of a just universe.

9   Sin and Evil

The preceding description of the best of all possible worlds may be taken by some as a typical instance of Leibniz's notorious philosophical 'optimism', an attitude maliciously described by Voltaire as 'the passion for insisting that everything is fine when one is wretched' (*126*, ch.19). 'Maliciously', in this case, because Leibniz never wished to deny the existence of evil, sin and misery; and the subject has been avoided so far merely because his treatment of it is easier to understand when the main system of his ideas is already known.

In fact, Leibniz has a good deal to say about what is generally called 'the problem of evil'. By far the fullest discussion of it is found in his *Theodicy*, a work that was hailed in its own day as a significant contribution to philosophical and theological thinking on the matter, and was extensively popularised by other writers (e.g. *21*). We shall examine the basis of his solution to the problem in Chapter 11, and for the present will merely detail the structure of his main arguments, since this will amplify the preceding discussion. It will be seen that Leibniz actually has two problems to solve: the first being that of how man can behave wrongly, given the natural inclinations of his will and reason toward the good; and the second, that of how sin and other forms of evil can occur in a world that is the best of all possible ones.

His proposed solution to the first problem must be seen within the context of his general account of human action. It will be recalled that the theory of volition implies that correct judgment necessarily results in right action: wrong behaviour, therefore, must be a consequence of an error of judgment, in which the lesser good is chosen instead of the greater. Leibniz accounts for this possibility in terms of a general definition of the nature of evil: 'perfection is a positive thing, an absolute reality; imperfection is privative, arising from limitation and leading to further privations' (G.vi.122). In the present context, this basic notion finds application in the thesis that man's intellect is necessarily finite, is therefore unable always to consider all the relevant factors to a judgment, and is consequently liable to make mistakes. He explains the issue as follows:

> Where does evil come from? . . . Its source must be sought in the concept of the creature, in the nature that is contained in the eternal truths in God's mind, independent of his will. One must recognise that there is an original imperfection in the creature, even before it sins, because it is essentially finite: this means that it cannot know everything, and can thus make mistakes and other errors. (G.vi.114)

The finitude of the human intellect is evidenced in the fact that our perceptions of the universe are less clear and orderly than God's, and this is associated with the limitations of the human body: for, believing that the mind is its 'connate idea', he remarks that 'the existence of a corrupted body is necessarily followed by a weakness in the faculties of the mind' (Gr.243). This should not be taken to imply a causal relationship; the physical and mental limitations of the creature result equally from its finite concept or 'essence', which forms a part of the concept of the world in which it figures.

Although this theory can serve to explain the possibility of an error of judgment, and thereby of a morally wrong action, it merely shifts the burden of accounting for its occurrence. In saying that man sins because he is created imperfect, Leibniz invites the question of why he was thus created; and this 'solution' to the first problem consequently makes it coalesce with the second, of how the best of all possible worlds can contain imperfections. His answer to this problem is fundamentally different from the argument just considered, since it consists in showing that it would have been impossible for God to have created a world utterly perfect in every respect. It must be remembered that God's creative act is merely a *fiat* of his will, actualising the idea of a world that is independently given in his understanding; and it is in this idea, in the 'region of eternal truths' as it is called at G.vi.115, that the 'ideal cause' of evil is to be found. Since this idea is merely that of the largest compossible set of possible entities, its intrinsic characteristics are determined not by God but by the logical test of non-contradiction, which is the criterion of possibility. The limitations in the idea of the world arise from this logical constraint. Leibniz is fond of comparing this situation with the presence of incommensurables in geometry, as he does at Gr.361; for instance, there is no exactly calculable proportion between the diameter and the circumference of a circle. The point of comparison is not merely that this can be interpreted as a kind of imperfection, but that the circle cannot exist without it. In the same fashion, he suggests at Gr.324, the concept of this world contains similar intrinsic imperfections, which must inevitably be realised in the creation.

This solution to the problem of evil is not without parallels in the thought of other philosophers. Bouillet has remarked that it is virtually identical with the solution proposed by Plotinus and St Augustine (46, 1.431), and it is highly possible that Leibniz derived the basic idea from them. More interesting is the fact that it is not radically different from the fundamental position of the Manichaean heresy, inasmuch as the necessities of logic are presented with the force of an 'evil principle' which circumscribes the benevolent intentions of God. There are places in Leibniz's writings where such an idea is quite apparent: at Gr.355, for instance, he observes that everything is composed of metaphysical 'form' and 'matter', and associates these respectively with good and evil in a manner that is strikingly reminiscent of Giordano Bruno's thesis of the 'coincidence of opposites' (98). But these remarks carry the danger of obscuring his real meaning. Riley, for example, comments that evil has the status of an 'essence' in Leibniz's system; and so one needs to bear in mind the observation at G.II.311, that evil can have no substantial reality whatsoever since it is essentially negative, a privation and a 'not-being'.

This basic conception of evil, since it is associated with Leibniz's general analysis of value, is discussed further in Chapter 11. But one may here forestall an objection that is commonly raised against it – by McCloskey, for instance (96, 189). He argues as follows: since pain is an acknowledged evil, and all evil is the privation of some good, pain must be regarded as the privation of happiness; but it is absurd to say that someone

who is suffering pain is simply not feeling happy; so this
reductio ad absurdum shows that the theory of evil must be
false. This objection entirely misses the point, as it takes a theory
that aims to show why pain is evil as a theory that tries to explain
what pain is. This can be seen if one grants McCloskey's contention that pain is a distinct and immediate sensation : one
is still left with the question of why this sensation is an evil. The
mere fact that it is unpleasant can scarcely be proposed as a
serious answer, as we well know that what we like or dislike
is by no means always the same as what we regard as good or
evil. Leibniz's general notion of evil (which he shared with
Scholastic philosophers) is therefore not intrinsically absurd, and
may be taken for the time being as an acceptable hypothesis in
his philosophy.

The thesis that imperfection is a necessary feature in the
concept of this world carries the important implication that
God cannot be held responsible or blameworthy for the occurrence of evil. For divine omnipotence does not include the
ability to resolve logical contradictions, and God, in creating
the world, is bound to create it as it is given to him by his understanding, imperfections and all. Nor does the presence of inherent
imperfections imply that it is other than the most perfect of the
possible worlds. As Mackie has observed (*93*, 206), one can
admit the presence of first-order evils (such as pain and sin) in
the world, and yet consistently maintain that it is good as a
whole in terms of some second-order criterion – as Leibniz does,
using his concept of harmony as the standard of cosmic goodness.
It is quite possible, of course, that some world that is less perfect
by that criterion might be wholly free of moral evil; but God
could not have created that one without conflicting with the
moral necessity arising from his own nature, as we have previously
seen. By this means Leibniz argues that God could not but
create a world containing imperfections :

> When the act is morally wrong, God can only will to permit
> it. The crime is not an end in itself, nor a means to an end;
> it is only a necessary condition, and therefore it is not directly
> willed for itself, as I have previously shown. And God could
> not prevent it without conflict with his duty to create the
> best, which would be far worse than the man's crime, and

which, as I have already commented, would destroy his divine character. God is therefore bound by a moral necessity, given in his own nature, to permit the moral evil of the beings whom he creates. (G.vi.204)

In thus arguing that God is not to be blamed for the limitations of his creation, Leibniz might be thought to lay himself open to the objection that men are not to be blamed for their sins either, since these arise from those limitations. The most famous instance of this criticism is Russell's claim that all these theories are 'discreditable subterfuges', designed to conceal the unwelcome fact that all moral evil is 'original sin' (*115*, 120). This view is incorrect, and it is important to see why. First, Leibniz is clearly not dealing with the orthodox doctrine of original sin, which is 'that every man . . . is born in a condition of disgrace and guilt, caused in him by the sin of the first man' (*53*, XII.275). He makes no mention of Adam, for the simple reason that Adam's sin was as much a result of his limitations as that of any other man. Nor does Leibniz maintain that man is culpable from the moment of his birth. It is freewill that is the immediate cause of guilt and punishment, and limitation is only the ultimate cause, as he says at G.vi.288 : so that he is not culpable until he has deliberately behaved wrongly. He likewise denies that limitation necessitates such behaviour, since that would remove the contingency that is the basis of freewill (Gr.413); the limitation merely makes the creature 'able to sin and act wrongly' (G.iv.455). In other words, it merely explains the fact of immoral behaviour :

No one can deny that every creature is essentially limited, for it is obvious that unless this is so no sin could occur. Its limitation accounts for its sin not as an unavoidable cause but merely as a necessary condition. If a free creature did not lack a certain degree of perfection it would not waver and yield to some temptation with which it is faced, and thus its freedom would never be wrongly employed. (*6*, 83)

Here we have an important and striking parallel with Leibniz's thesis of psychological determinism discussed in Chapter 3. Just as that aimed merely to ensure that an explanation could be given for every voluntary act, so his theory of metaphysical limitation merely seeks to account for the fact that such acts can be morally wrong. And just as it was observed that his determinism threatens freedom, so limitation makes the possibility of absolute virtue a very remote one. It is here that one sees the grain of truth in Russell's criticism, for Leibniz betrays more than a hint of sympathy with Calvinist ideas in thinking human sin is both probable and ultimately inexplicable. He comments, for instance, that 'the question why God gave this spirit more perfection than that one' is unanswerable, since the whole matter is a mystery (E.670); and he claims that divine favour is not always given in this life when it is deserved, and certainly cannot be ensured by 'prayers, good intentions, and virtuous behaviour' (G.1.360). At one point (E.72) he admittedly says that a man is not punished if he acted with good motives, but since this is a mere copy of Descartes' remark at AT.iv.266 it may be discounted.[11] Their limitation consequently implies that the vast majority of spirits, at any rate, will sin from time to time, and this must inevitably bring upon them a degree of unpleasantness and eventual punishment by God.

This conclusion adds the darker shades to the picture of the best of the possible worlds, which would otherwise be ludicrously bright and cheerful. One can see that Leibnizian optimism in fact amounts to no more than confidence in the goodness of God,

11. Leibniz's comment on this matter occurs in his *De Vita Beata*, which has been shown by Trendelenburg to be entirely a selection of excerpts from Descartes' letters, translated into Latin and loosely connected with one another. He has published a 'parallel text' of the whole, displaying the close correspondences, at *124*, Bd.2.

In a letter to Foucher at A.ii.i.247, Leibniz says that he had not read Descartes before his visit to Paris in 1672; but this must refer to the metaphysical and mathematical works, since he claims to have read the letters on moral philosophy in a letter to Van Velthuysen of 1670 (A.ii.i.39). He is probably referring to the three-volume edition of Descartes' correspondence (Amsterdam, 1668), and Erdmann is probably right in dating the *De Vita Beata* to around 1669 (in the preface to his edition).

Grua has observed that Descartes' thoughts on ethics are largely an appendage to the rest of his philosophy, so that they could easily be excerpted with little trace of their origin (*66*, 138). They do not wholly coincide with Leibniz's ideas – there is, for instance, no mention of the definition of love in the work, which appears in his other writings of that time. I have felt free to refer to the work when it is confirmed elsewhere by Leibniz but, as in the present instance, to discount it when it is not.

and the belief that he acted as well as he could within the constraints of logical necessity. For, as Lovejoy has put it, 'to assert that this is the best of all possible worlds implies nothing as to the absolute goodness of this world; it implies only that any other world which is metaphysically capable of existence would be worse' (*89, 921*). This is yet another instance of the intriguing fact that Leibniz's most positive assertions are frequently employed in a mainly negative role: it was shown in Chapter 5 that his thesis of egoism merely ensures that the agent will not voluntarily harm himself; so here he has no wish to deny the existence of manifold evils in the best of all worlds. We shall see in the next chapter how Leibniz thought that some of these evils could be mitigated.

Having developed the ethical system that has been outlined in the preceding pages, it would have been open to Leibniz, like Plato (*Republic*, 472c), to have argued that the philosopher is not obliged to go further and show how his ethical ideals are to be realised in practice. But as a matter of fact (and again like Plato) Leibniz had many schemes for the implementation of his ideas, a brief discussion of which will serve to clarify further just what his moral system involves.

Leibniz's reasons for this practical concern are really twofold, deriving in the first place from his personal outlook and ambition. It must not be forgotten that he always wanted to be a man of affairs; in 1667, for instance, he threw up the chance of an academic career in order to be legal adviser to the Elector of Mainz; and though the circumstances of his life thereafter largely frustrated his hopes of active involvement in politics, he always retained a practical interest in matters of state. The second reason was no doubt his sheer humanity. Born in 1646 at the close of the Thirty Years' War, he was horrified by the strife and dissension that raged in Europe almost continuously until his death in 1716; and he recognised the supreme need for peace and a proper regulation of international affairs. Some of his more interesting schemes to this end are reproduced by Riley (*113*), and make fascinating reading. In accord with all these hopes, Leibniz wrote of the need for 'a more practical work, on how our knowledge should be implemented' (C.354), and though he never found time to write it, his works are scattered with remarks on the problem. His personal motto, likewise, was *Theoria cum praxi* ('Theory with practice'). And in what is probably his strongest statement of the idea, he writes that 'God has no use for armchair philosophers, for theoretical works and academic speculations' (OH.95); instead, the philosopher must involve himself in practical affairs, and make real use of his knowledge of the truth.

As we have previously seen, Leibniz conceives morality and right conduct as a means to the attainment of happiness. Happiness is defined as a state of continual pleasure, which must consist in 'a constant progress towards greater perfection' (G.II.136), through the theory of pleasure itself. This can be seen as the satisfaction of an unceasing desire, for he writes that 'a cessation of desire, a situation in which you wish for nothing, is not happiness but torpor' (A.VI.i.466). This remark is clearly intended to express his disagreement with the Stoic conception of happiness which involved such freedom from desire; and at the same time, it indicates his close agreement with the Hobbesian concept (R.44). Hobbes had been led to this idea through his belief that 'life itself is but motion, and can never be without desire' (R.37), and a similar idea is obviously present in Leibniz's use of *conatus* as the essence of mind, as was shown in Chapter 2. This carries the important implication that happiness, though it is perceived at a conscious level, is nevertheless founded upon a metaphysical development of the individual's nature, a progress towards its perfection and fulfilment. So Leibniz can describe happiness in dispositional terms, writing that 'it is quite sufficient for a man to feel joy in his condition as often as he thinks about it' (E.671).

With this ideal of happiness proposed as the end, Leibniz advances his moral theory as the means to it. In his more practical schemes, this theory is further developed in the three main areas of Religion, Politics and Education.

The significance of religion arises initially from a problem caused by the notion of happiness itself. For how is it possible for a finite creature to make infinite progress towards perfection? The answer to this is provided by the thesis that God is infinite in perfection, and therefore the knowledge of God must involve continuing pleasure since the perception of such perfection can never be complete (G.VI.606). By 'knowledge' in this context, Leibniz naturally does not mean total comprehension; it is quite sufficient, he says, to have a meaningful idea of God as supremely wise and powerful (OH.94). The correspondence of such an idea with a real entity is ensured not merely by logical proofs of God's existence, but even more by the similarity in nature between

God and the spirits. At G.vi.507, for instance, it is claimed that we, like God, are able to recognise the order in the world about us and reproduce this in the management of our affairs; and likewise our perceptions correspond more or less with those of God (G.vi.121). This metaphysical continuity is the basis for Leibniz's description of our perfection as a 'kind of participation in God' (G.vii.148), a remark whose Platonic tone is taken up again in the following :

> Every perfection derives directly from God . . . These divine perfections are shared by all creatures, and are to be found in even the most insignificant. In every substance there is something of the infinite, an imprint or representation of God's omnipotence and omniscience. (Gu.i.410)

It is noteworthy that views were held by Leibniz's contemporaries that were only verbally similar to this. We find that Spinoza, for example, writes of the 'dependence' of all things on God (S.iii.23), but wishes to express by this the purely ontological thesis that God is the reason for their continued existence (S.i.57). Though Leibniz could also have held such a view, he prefers to present his theory as a way of picturing the spirits' fulfilment of happiness in God, as when he writes that 'God's perfection is somehow dispensed upon us by being known and loved' (M.21).

It will be apparent that this theory necessitates a special interpretation of the 'love' that is borne toward God. We have seen that love for other men is a matter of active benevolence, a practical effort to increase their perfection and happiness; but this is clearly impossible as regards God, since the divine perfection is absolute and cannot be increased (Gr.95). The love of God must therefore be primarily a matter of contemplation, whence unending happiness may be derived (Gr.8). But only primarily so : for Leibniz maintains that such contemplation must lead to a wholehearted involvement in the moral life. He argues that one cannot love God without 'willing what he wills', and thus trying to emulate his universal justice (M.74). For in loving God, one is made particularly mindful of his creative benevolence, and this gives rise to a disposition to love every man simply as a rational being created like oneself, which is the basis of justice (M.37). As Leibniz comments, 'it is therefore the case that one cannot love God without loving one's fellow-man' (Gr.581).

He is somewhat scornful of thinkers who 'reduce religion to mere morality' (A.ii.i.302), and this must be borne in mind when considering the ethical implications of his ideas on religion. He insists, at M.6, that this life is of little significance when compared with the life to come, and he clearly thought that the happiness to be derived from the mere knowledge and worship of God was of the utmost importance. Nevertheless, religion leads naturally to moral virtue. At Gr.107, for example, he makes mention of the commandment 'that ye love one another, as I have loved you' (John, xv.12) as being the touchstone of true religion; and further stresses the similarity with the Christian message by commenting that justice is 'brotherly love' (G.vii. 75). Moreover, he gives his concern with religion a more practical application. He recognised that many of the political dissensions of his time were intimately associated with religious divisions, especially between Protestants and Catholics; and therefore felt that religious agreement must be a necessary precondition of civil peace. By 1670, he had already set himself the task of establishing 'the truth of natural religion' (D.v.345), proving the existence of God and the immortality of the soul, and thence deriving the basic principles of religion and morality in which all rational men would have to agree. It will be clear that his moral system is at least partly designed to this end; at D.v.118, for instance, he sets out its basic theories, and expresses the hope that they 'will perhaps help to bring an end to strife, at least to some degree'.

Leibniz's natural religion is founded, like his ethics, upon the notion of love and charity, and is therefore called a 'catholic' faith:

The basis of true communion in the body of Christ is charity; and all men who promote division, by setting obstacles in the path of reconciliation, schismatics. Those on the other hand who are willing to do what they can to promote unity are catholics. These are undeniable and all-important principles. (D.v.550)

Upon this basis he proposed the idea of a world-wide society, the 'Christian Brotherhood', which would combine the functions of Church and State, and comprehend all men in a truly just scheme of social organisation (M.11). In other words, it was to realise in human society the characteristics of the Kingdom of Grace, in which the basic principle is that of love, and in which virtue is always rewarded (M.20). The basic idea of this clearly has affinities with St Augustine's ideal of the 'City of God' (*41*); but whereas that was an other-worldly conception, Leibniz's was intended as a practical possibility, the plans for it being given in a work of 1677 written under his pseudonym of 'Caesarinus Fürstenerius' (*5, IV*). A useful summary of it, and an important comment on it, is given by Fontenelle :

> He would have it that all the christian states, at least those in the West, comprise a single body, of which the Pope and the Emperor are the spiritual and temporal heads respectively. . . . This christian realm would not have been a surprising idea for a German Catholic, but Leibniz was a Lutheran : in religion, his partisan affiliation was quite overcome by his supreme desire for organisation. (*55*)

It is interesting that Tschirnhaus, who met Leibniz in Paris in 1675, was also struck by the fact that 'he had none of the common theological prejudices' (S.II.407) – clearly, he lived up to the standards he advocated.

Thus the concern with religion, initially dealing with the knowledge of God, leads to a concern with politics and government. Leibniz was a prolific writer on this subject, and many of his schemes lack the religious overtones of the foregoing; it will be sufficient here to mention only their basic ideas, since Riley deals with his political thought in full. They all develop the basic idea of an 'unlimited unequal society', that is, one which comprehends all areas of political intercourse and social life, and which is based upon the natural inequalities between men. He contends that such a society must have two aims : a minimal one, of ensuring that no harm comes to any of its members; and a maximal one, of helping its members to live as happily as possible (Gr.613). These obviously remind us of the principles of natural justice, and the first in particular relates to Leibniz's

concern for the establishment of peace, which was shared also by
Kant (*110*, 93). The fundamental principle upon which such a
society is to be run is likewise that of the universal justice displayed by God, that of securing the greatest welfare for all (M.3).
It should be noted that this represents a slightly different
criterion from that used by later Utilitarian thinkers. For he
claims that the 'common good' is the collection of individual
goods into a 'single whole', in which the magnitude of each is
as important as their number (M.86); and this suggests that
the welfare of the majority is not to be secured at the expense of
that of a minority, a conclusion reinforced by the basic precepts
of natural justice.

As such a concern for political reform suggests, the fact that
he believed religion and morality to be closely connected did not
prevent Leibniz from presenting his ideas in a wholly secular
context. This is further apparent in his ideas on education. His
concern with this issue derives initially from the importance of
reason and wisdom as the means whereby one is enabled to behave
virtuously. Now wisdom is simply an increase in organised knowledge, which comprises the imposition of order upon a number
of facts : in other words, an exact parallel with the harmony of
the world. He writes, for instance, that 'that is a more perfect
manner of knowing, in which a number of things are simul-
taneously known together' (Gr.13). This premiss yields three
significant conclusions. In the first place, it follows that all new
knowledge will constitute an increase in the perfection of the
individual, and will therefore be pleasurable for him (Gu.37).
Secondly, it implies that the mind of the wise man will be like
a microcosm of the universe, and will mirror its harmony and
order – again, a pleasant thing (E.672). And thirdly, it means
that the individual will be morally good, since volition is intimately
linked with the intellect. Leibniz writes that there is a
'beauty' in virtue, residing in the proportion between power
and understanding, which is perfected in the balance between
God's omnipotence and omniscience (A.iv.i.531). In the same
way, a man will be truly happy when 'he is able to do what he
wants and knows to be right' (M.22) : an idea that is restated,
with a deliberate echo of the doctrine of the moral qualities, as a
man 'doing everything that it is possible for him to do' (A.iv.i.
530).

In similar words, Hutcheson writes that 'that must be the perfection of virtue, where the moment of good produced equals the ability' (R.337). For these reasons, therefore, the acquisition of knowledge and wisdom comes to be of great importance in a practical context, as providing pleasure in itself and as making the individual virtuous.

In accord with this belief, Leibniz was extremely (and quite justifiably) critical of the new scientific societies that had been created in London and Paris. For he pointed out that the experiments they performed were random and inconsequential, producing a host of unexplained and unrelated facts (A.II.i.181); and their members were therefore like 'a band of men, marching in confusion in the dark' (G.VII.157). Despite their academic calibre, they were not adding to the sum of human knowledge since they were not organising their research and discoveries. He therefore produced several plans for a new society (reviewed at 51, appx.4), in which he stressed the importance of systematic research, and above all the need for interdisciplinary contact and consultation, in order to relate the various branches of enquiry to one another. This plan, at any rate, did reach fulfilment within his lifetime. The Berlin Academy of Sciences was founded in 1700 on this model, with Leibniz as its first proud president.

Yet such an academy was only a part of the total scheme. In the first place, it was to include the study of theology and metaphysics, and many other branches of knowledge, as well as that of the physical sciences (C.153). And secondly, it was to take in pupils for instruction, to help realise his moral and social ideals. For he says that the very fact that men will do so much to attain unworthy ends through debased ambition gives him cause to hope that they will do even more in pursuit of high ideals, once acquainted with their worth (G.v.177): perhaps a pious hope, but one that is nevertheless the basic creed of many educationists. The pupils and their teachers were to live in a largely closed community, sharing a simple and austere life of study and brotherhood – an idea that owed much to the ancient sect of Pythagorean philosophers, as Leibniz acknowledged (G.VII.147). And there was to be little formal instruction: the main job was research and the advancement of knowledge, with the pupils aspiring to emulate their teachers because of the admiration that came from associating with such men of learning and virtue (E.671).

Lest it be thought that this is a fanciful idea, it is worth pointing out that it has been put into practice throughout the world : for it is the basic concept upon which every modern university is founded. It is an educational ideal that is far different from the medieval conception, in which the student was expected to assimilate a static body of approved knowledge, and which was still the norm in Leibniz's day. The first attempt to realise his idea occurred twenty years after his death, with the foundation of the University of Göttingen in 1736 (*125*); since then, of course, it has spread far and wide.

11   Value and Perfection

During the course of the preceding chapters, a number of concepts have been encountered that are regarded by Leibniz as being in some way endowed with value. Such, for instance, are the object of volition, virtuous activity, the harmony of the world, and perfection generally; and, in a negative context, moral evil and imperfection. The present chapter comprises the long-awaited attempt to draw these diverse threads together, and to explain the fundamental theory of value that underlies the whole ethical system. It must be said, however, that the argument presented here is a hypothetical reconstruction. For Leibniz never explains his basic analysis of value, and indeed offers only the slightest and most scattered hints as to its nature; perhaps because such conceptual analysis was not the philosophical vogue that it has later become; and perhaps also because his theory, as we shall see, has continuities with the prevalent Scholastic system, and therefore he assumed that it would be familiar to his readers. The following reconstruction, then, can be regarded as valid only inasmuch as it helps to clarify a number of obscure points in the system previously discussed.

The few definitions of value that Leibniz does produce generally take the form of that previously encountered, in which the three concepts of moral, physical and metaphysical good are successively defined. These should not be taken to represent three distinct senses of the word 'good', but merely three applications of it, each dealing with a different 'sphere of discourse' as it were. It seems to have been the fashion to employ this tripartite scheme, since almost every major concept in Chauvin's *Lexicon* (*50*) is defined in the same three ways. The three things which Leibniz defines as good are perfection, pleasure, and just conduct. They form an explanatory hierarchy, in the sense that the value of a just action is founded on the fact that it produces pleasure, and this in turn is explained in terms of its effect in increasing the perfection of the agent. Consequently, the whole burden of this scheme is laid upon the concept of metaphysical perfection, and the question arises of why this is to be regarded as good.

This question is necessarily unanswerable within the triple scheme of concepts given by Leibniz; but it may be answered in terms of two other concepts which, since he makes no mention of them, one may call the ideas of Generic and Beneficial goodness. The concept of generic goodness is that of something's being *good of its kind* : if 'X' be taken to stand for the name of a certain kind of thing, it may be represented in English by the statement 'this X is good as an X' – or, to put it more briefly, 'this is a good X'. It is a recognisable idea, though it is seldom used. The concept of beneficial goodness, on the other hand, is frequently encountered : it is that of being good in the sense of serving to improve, benefit or ameliorate, and may be represented by 'this is good for an X'. The phrases 'good as' and 'good for' thus roughly represent the distinction between the two concepts. As Kant observed (K.v.59), these are represented by different words in German but by the single word *bonum* in Latin – a limitation of vocabulary that may help to explain the fact that Leibniz did not use the concepts. But it is arguable that he could well have done so : generic goodness, for instance, would seem to apply to the perfected state of the individual spirit, which has been set up as the goal of the moral life. The beneficial good likewise makes its appearance as the object of volition, divided, as was seen in Chapter 2, into the 'real' and 'apparent' good, of which only the former will necessarily benefit the agent who attains it.

The concept of beneficial goodness can already serve to explain one obscure point in Leibniz's thought : namely, the assumption that an increase in perfection will be accompanied by the sensation of pleasure. For such an increase will inevitably help to make the monad more perfect, and must therefore be good for it; whence it is plausible to suggest that it will be enjoyed, particularly when its beneficial effect is known. Of course, this still does not 'prove' a necessary connection between pleasure and perfection, and indeed it may well be impossible to do so; but it at least makes this postulate more comprehensible, and disposes us to accept it more readily.

However, the concept of generic goodness is more important since it underpins that of beneficial goodness, explaining why a state of perfection is itself good. It is also more difficult to comprehend, being rather obscure in its own right, and being analysed in terms of perfection. We shall first consider this latter doctrine.

The idea of 'a perfection' is not an intrinsically difficult notion : it is that of a single positive quality that can be possessed in a maximal degree (G.vii.261). For example, the attributes of power and knowledge count as perfections, but those of number and size do not : for neither of the latter can be said to be 'greatest' in any intelligible sense (G.iv.427). As such, perfections are merely the counterparts of the various predicates that go to make up the complete concept of an individual substance, which was discussed in Chapter 4 : just as, in logical terms, its concept is said to be composed of predicates, so, in metaphysical ones, its 'essence' is composed of perfections. Leibniz further maintains that the complexity of such an essence, or such a concept, is the same thing as its 'reality' (G.i.266). By this, he does not mean that a simple essence is less real, in the sense of less actual, than one that is complex; the idea is exactly that expressed by Kant, when he wrote that 'the more truths implied by a given concept, the more criteria there are for its objective reality' (K.iii.98). In other words, an essence that has great reality will have many predicates, considered as a concept, and many qualities, considered as an existent. So Leibniz writes as follows :

> Essence is distinct conceivability, and existence is distinct perceivability . . . By 'distinct', I mean that it is clear enough, so that one can see that no contradiction is involved. Perfection is a degree of essence : what has more essence or reality is more perfect. (BH.123)

As the last sentence indicates, 'more perfect' means that the essence as a whole contains a greater number of 'perfections' – the distinction between adjective and noun is important if confusion is to be avoided. Leibniz accordingly says that 'in this metaphysical sense' a man who is suffering pain is 'more perfect' than one who has no sensations at all (G.i.230). The same idea is expressed by the notion of things having 'more reality', in accordance with Spinoza's assertion that this describes their possession of more attributes (S.1.42). Finally, there is yet another comparative standard, that of 'intension', which describes the degree to which a quality is exhibited (G.1.228): an essence with greater intension will include more of its constituent qualities, as one with greater reality will have a larger number of them. Leibniz frequently uses the phrase 'more perfect' to cover both intension and reality.

To understand these ideas further, and to see how they might be related to the notion of value, it will be helpful to consider a simple example. Let it be assumed that there are only three qualities which a man must possess if he is to be a carpenter: namely, that he can distinguish various kinds of wood, that he knows how to construct joints, and that he can use his tools with safety and efficiency. These three qualities will then constitute the 'essence' of a carpenter, for there is no difference between knowing what something is and knowing its essence, as Aristotle says (*10*, 1031b): they form a set of criteria that is both necessary and sufficient for a man's *being* a carpenter. This essence has greater reality than the essence of a lumberjack, say, since the lumberjack does not need to know how to construct joints, although he must have the other two qualities; his essence is therefore less complex than that of a carpenter. Now if the essence of the carpenter has greater intension, all these qualities will be present in a greater degree: he will be more adept at telling one wood from another, will know how to build a greater number of joints, and will be more skilful with his tools. In consequence, he will clearly be better as a carpenter: in other words, he will have greater generic goodness than the mere beginner or apprentice.

Although this example suggests a plausible connection between the notion of value and Leibniz's concepts of perfection, it illustrates three important points. First, if he is going to use 'more perfect' to mean 'better' with any legitimacy, it must express the notion of greater intension rather than that of greater reality. For there is no clear reason why complexity should, *per se*, be connected with value, any more than there is for saying that carpenters are 'better' than lumberjacks. It will be seen that Leibniz does not always abide by this rule. Secondly, it shows that the 'better' carpenter is not, as is sometimes thought, simply the man who is 'better at his job' – his value does not derive solely from his efficiency in fulfilling his function. For the reason why he does his job better is because he possesses the given qualities in a greater degree, and this latter criterion is thus logically prior. His function is certainly important as pointing to the defining criteria of a carpenter, but does not bestow value of itself. And finally, it illustrates the difficulty of defining the notion of a 'kind', which lies at the root of generic goodness. For the good carpenter may also be a bad instructor or husband; the example given only works because we have arbitrarily defined the genus under which the man is to be considered. But Leibniz seems to think that the 'kinds' are given in nature, in the very concepts of the individuals concerned; and this, as we shall see, raises considerable difficulties for his system.

For the present, however, it should be noted that the scheme implies a correspondence between value and ontology, which is most clearly demonstrated by the concept of God as both supremely good and supremely perfect. The latter fact is expressed in the idea that he possesses a maximum of reality (Gr.11), having all perfections in his essence, and in the idea that he is 'the greatest in intension of perfection' (G.iv.511), since all the perfections are present in a maximal degree. God can thus properly be described as 'infinite', since the only limitations on his being are purely logical ones (G.vi.613). Other monads, however, are 'limited' in the sense of not having so many qualities to such a degree, and are therefore theoretically definable by reference to the concept of God : a point observed by Kant, when he claimed that all things could be defined by the predicates they lack, in comparison with 'the totality of all possible predicates' (K.iii.385). The same idea is found when Leibniz writes of the way things are composed of 'perfection and limitation', and compares this with their creation 'out of God and nothing', and the generation of numbers out of 1 and 0 in the binary calculus that he had developed (Gr.371). Probably, the idea also lies behind his thoughts on the 'dependence' or 'participation' of the creation vis-à-vis God, since they are not only ontologically but also conceptually derived from God. However, Leibniz and Kant disagree concerning the existence of God. Leibniz had adopted the ontological proof of God's existence derived from St Anselm, with the single modification of showing that the concept of 'the most perfect being' does not involve logical contradiction. Kant criticises this at K.III.399, observing that a possible idea does not ensure the possibility of an existent; and, in the light of his thorough critique of the ontological proof, one must admit that Leibniz fails to demonstrate the existence of God in this way.

The remarks on limitation in the preceding paragraph serve to explain Leibniz's theory of evil, which was left incomplete in Chapter 9. For it has been shown that limitation expresses the mere absence of a quality, the lack of a possible perfection : it is Kant's concept of a 'transcendental negation' which expresses a 'not-being in itself' (K.III.387). As such, it is entirely different from the notion of evil, which was traditionally defined as the 'privation of good' (ST.Ia, 48.5). The difference between the concepts is explained by Suarez :

> As regards the distinction between the other pair of terms, namely privation and negation, it is clear that they are different in this respect : negation merely signifies a lack in a subject, while privation signifies a lack in a subject naturally fitted to have what it lacks. (62, 382)

Thus Leibniz argues that the limitations of the human intellect lead to mistakes in conduct which bring unhappiness : and since this is contrary to the happiness that man is 'naturally fitted' to achieve, it is a privation and therefore evil. It is clear that the argument rests upon a concealed tautology. A privation is essentially something that would not be the case if everything were as it should be, and it thus includes intrinsic connotations of 'badness' or failure. It is an evaluative term, and may be applied equally at the 'physical' level of pleasure and pain as well as at the underlying 'metaphysical' level of perfection and imperfection. By contrast, the notion of limitation is purely descriptive, since it expresses no more than the idea of negation. When Leibniz asserts that man is essentially limited, he in fact means no more than that man is not God, since the human essence contains less reality or complexity than the divine : he does not mean that man is essentially evil, or somehow lacking a perfection that he should naturally have.

The opposite of privation is the state of being perfect – of 'being as much as it is possible to be' (A.vi.ii.494), or as Aristotle put it more clearly, of 'not lacking any part of a natural magnitude [i.e., reality]' (*10*, 1021b). Thus the contrast between good and evil is fully displayed, since the state of being perfect is that of being generically good. But the close relation between value and essence again raises some fundamental problems. In the first place, Leibniz would presumably wish to assert that the spirits have more reality than the beasts, since they alone possess the perfection of rationality. If so, however, this would conflict with his belief that every substance has an infinitely complex concept: for this implies that they are all equal in reality. This difficulty might perhaps be overcome by saying that they are not equally complex as regards the primitive predicates in their concepts, for some substances have more intrinsic predicates than others; the 'infinity' comes in only with the deduction of derivative predicates, through the laws of the pre-established harmony. If so, this would still have the important implication that the spirits cannot be said to be 'better' than the beasts, any more than the carpenter is better than the lumberjack. For they are different things, and comparisons of value can only be made between things of the same kind. So Leibniz might attempt to deal with the problem of 'kinds' by pointing out that all spirits, for example, share the same basic properties of reason and volition: they are therefore of the same kind, and the spirit that develops its rationality more than the others, which increases the intension of its essential qualities, is therefore 'more perfect' and better than the rest.

There is some doubt, however, whether even this is possible. The concept of perfection with which he is working is that called 'transcendental' by Kant, and described by him as 'the completeness of each thing by reference to its own kind' (K.v.41); and Spinoza, using the same concept, observed that there is a good sense in which the perfection of a thing is coextensive with its essence (for it has just the qualities which it does have), so that everything, 'considered in itself', is perfect (S.ii.253). Now a similar conclusion might seem to follow from Leibniz's premisses. His principle of the Identity of Indiscernibles implies that the concept or essence of every monad is unique: and since none of them can consequently be compared with another, each of them must be perfect in itself. There are, in fact, as many 'kinds' as there are monads, and there is no sound reason why, as suggested above, one should regard only the most basic and general qualities as the defining criteria of a 'kind'. Leibniz has only one possible rejoinder to this. It is open to him to argue that it would still be possible to judge the intension of an individual's qualities, the extent to which a given spirit has succeeded in developing the unique set of perfections with which it started life. Although comparisons of value may be impossible to make, it is still the case that evaluative statements have meaning : and to say that a man is 'better' than he was would mean that he is on the way to fulfilling his natural potentialities. It is interesting to note that Goethe later made considerable use of such a notion of 'self-realisation' as the goal of life, and supposedly derived it from his reading of Leibniz.

Without attempting to minimise the conceptual problems involved in such an effort to link value with perfection, it can at least be said that Leibniz has thus provided a workable sense in which a substance can be described as more or less perfect, and that it is not implausible to relate this with a description of it as 'better' or 'worse'. This reveals that his basic theory is not as unsound as is sometimes supposed, and that it can escape some of the criticisms that have been levelled against it. Broad, for instance, has written that 'there is one and only one sense in which the words "perfect" and "imperfect" can properly and literally be used, and that is "realising or falling short of the intentions of the designer" ' (47, 44). Now it is certainly true that such teleological interpretation does play an important role in Leibniz's thought; in regarding the world as fulfilling God's purposes, for instance, or in making the criterion of virtue that of 'success' in choosing and carrying out the most pleasant course of action. But it needs also to be noticed that this mode of interpretation is not of primary importance. For both the purposes of God and the 'right' actions of a spirit are determined by the metaphysical nature of the individual concerned : the proper 'function' of each is a consequence of its essence, and is not arbitrarily chosen by the will.

This important fact leads directly to an elucidation of the necessary 'moral truths', which have been mentioned more than once in the preceding chapters. It can now be seen that the essence of a spirit determines its generic good, the perfected state which it is fitted to achieve, and which it must presumably desire to achieve through the *conatus* that characterises its nature. The essence also determines its beneficial good; that is, the course of conduct that will bring the desired increase in the intension of its qualities, and thereby achieve its end. In this way, there is generated an indefinite number of statements about what it is right or wrong for the spirit to do, which are the 'moral necessities' involved in Leibniz's theory of duty. For these are necessary truths: like the very concept of the spirit itself they are 'eternal', and are merely understood by the mind of God in the process of creation. Thus the whole scheme of moral standards depends entirely upon logic. For the laws of logic alone determine the concepts of possible individuals, the moral ends which those individuals must seek to attain, and the means by which they must attain them if they are created.

Although this is a very significant conclusion for Leibniz's moral system, it raises a further and more fundamental problem for his theory of value. For if the whole scheme depends entirely upon the laws of logic and the concept of 'a perfection' (which, as has been shown, is not in itself evaluative), what guarantee is there that the prescribed state of being perfect will actually be good? It is certainly assumed that this will be the case, by other philosophers as well as Leibniz. Discussing Aristotle's idea of value as the realisation of potential, for example, Passmore has noted that potentialities were supposed to be 'for good' (*105*, 19), but this is far from being obviously the case. Leibniz has only one comment that might help, and that is his definition of a perfection as a *positive* quality. By this, he cannot intend a contrast with the concept of privation, since that would produce an obviously circular argument: he must mean it as the opposite of limitation or negation. This is the interpretation offered by Kant, who claims that only predicates which express a 'transcendental affirmation' can represent 'realities', and that all other predicates are mere negations of them, giving as examples the fact that poverty is a lack of wealth and ignorance an absence of knowledge (K.iii.387).

If this is what Leibniz also means, it is clear that he can

plausibly claim that many positive qualities will also be good and desirable; besides the examples given by Kant, stupidity and deceitfulness can be represented as the negative counterparts of wisdom and honesty. It is noteworthy that this is not an arbitrary classification: deceiving someone involves telling false-hoods, and falsity can rightly be regarded as the negation of truth since it is philosophically more simple to define it in that way, rather than truth in terms of falsity. But not all positive qualities necessarily follow this model. It is not clear, for instance, that being vain is necessarily to be understood as not being modest; nor is it clear that selfishness is the negation of benevo-lence, since it might be argued that it is simpler to define benevo-lence in terms of a lack of selfishness. If this is so, however, disastrous results ensue. For since God comprehends every positive quality, he may well be supremely selfish and vain as well as being honest and wise; and this not only involves a certain degree of contradiction, but must vitiate Leibniz's ethical scheme. Inasmuch as he fails to explain the notion of a positive quality, and how this yields the fact that it is good and desirable, he therefore leaves his theory of value resting on seriously weak foundations.

By way of conclusion to this chapter, it will perhaps be helpful to summarise the main points that have arisen. It has been seen that the general notion of perfection is twofold: it covers not only the concept of reality, or the number of qualities in a given essence; but also the concept of intension, or the degree to which such qualities are developed. It appears that the latter concept is more important, in that the general notion of an individual's increasing its intension seems to correspond with what we might call its 'improvement' or becoming 'better'. The concept of value here employed is what has been named that of generic goodness, the notion of its being better in itself, of improving as an individual of a certain kind. This concept serves as the foundation for that of beneficial goodness, which not only explains Leibniz's theories of evil and the moral truths but also accounts for his relating together moral virtue, pleasure, and increased perfection. To the extent that these concepts help to explain a number of fundamental points in his ethical system, they may be regarded as possessing a certain hypothetical validity. But it must be stressed that Leibniz provides no more than the most isolated comments on all these topics; that what he does say on them is frequently confused, obscure and self-contradictory; and that there remain several unsolved weaknesses in this scheme of ideas, which have been mentioned previously.

A number of criticisms have been made of Leibniz's ethical theories in the course of the preceding chapters. Now that the exposition of his moral system is complete, there remain some points to be made about the whole, and a general assessment of its significance needs to be attempted.

It will be fully apparent that the assertions with which this book began, regarding Leibniz's own interest in moral philosophy, are amply justified. The ethical system which he develops is extensive and complete, and is intrinsically related with his ideas on religion and social government; and not only is it expounded in a multitude of works dating from all periods of his life, as the references testify, but it is also closely connected with his metaphysics. Indeed, there are several points at which a consideration of his ethical purposes can help one to understand his metaphysical theory. For example, they explain why he divided the universe of monads into the two realms of Nature and Grace, how the scale of perfection is related to that of moral value, and what he means by the 'necessity' of God's creating the best of all possible worlds. Such an explanatory power is not surprising when it is remembered that the fundamentals of the ethical theory were already laid in 1671, whereas the monadology was not complete until 1686: his metaphysical system was worked out within the framework of his moral ideas, and was partly intended to serve as a foundation for them.

His moral ideas themselves are mainly meta-ethical in character, providing a system of concepts by means of which the realities of the moral life may be understood. As considered in this study, they begin with the psychology of ethics, in which the nature of volition and the possibility of free action are explained; from these there is developed the basic notion of right action as it concerns the individual, including the nature of duty; and finally this is extended to involve the whole of human society and all the spirits within the kingdom of grace. For the most part, the main ideas and principles are fairly simple and easily understood. The most notable exceptions to this general rule are those which look like positive assertions but which in fact serve as negative principles – instances that have been noted are the principle that the agent always seeks his own good and the assertion that this is the best of all possible worlds, both of which are employed by Leibniz with the main purpose of ruling out various possibilities.

Probably the most important fact about the ethical system as a whole is that it is really a combination of two distinct schemes. At the most fundamental level, there is a multitude of logically necessary moral truths which prescribe the moral obligations of every possible individual. These truths are wholly objective and absolute; they underlie the notions of moral virtue, duty, and the agent's 'real' good; and it is the task of reason and wisdom to discover them. At a subordinate level, Leibniz provides a system of ideas to generate a useful psychological inducement to live as such truths prescribe, focused upon the notions of pleasure and desire. This operates both by ensuring that all right action is pleasant for the agent, and by holding out the certainty that God will eventually reward him for his virtue. In other words, the two parts of the whole system relate to the elements of reason and desire in the individual, which shows how complete and well organised is his whole moral philosophy.

Its completeness is further demonstrated by the fact that even God himself is bound by the necessities of the moral law. It is seldom recognised that this was an extremely bold assertion on Leibniz's part : very few of his predecessors would have dared to argue that the standards of God's conduct are wholly independent of his will, as Leibniz maintains. But he saw that if God is going to be included in a system of ethics, as the creator of the world and as the dispenser of rewards and punishments, it is of the utmost importance that his moral standards should be the same as those of mankind. Because of this, he can rightly maintain the confidence in the justice and benevolence of God's management of things that is so often apparent in his works. Of course, this further demonstrates the primacy of the objective moral truths in his system.

The independence and primacy of such truths, however, do

give to the system a character that is perhaps not entirely desirable in modern eyes. For they absolutely prescribe the 'right' course of action for every individual, the series of actions which he must perform if he is to become perfect and happy. His aim should be to discern this course by his reason, and then totally to subordinate his will to its dictates, effecting that coincidence of moral and physical necessity that is the acme of virtue. The implication of this is that the agent is not free to choose his own destiny, to decide what he ought to make of himself, which some might regard as extremely undesirable. Leibniz, of course, would deny that this conflicts with the agent's freedom of action; and rightly so, for he is presumably able, and indeed liable, to stray from this path mapped out for him. And he would also point out that his actions are spontaneous and intelligent, that they serve to realise his true possibilities, and therefore he must be regarded as 'free'. But it is interesting to note that Kant thought that the agent should impose moral necessities upon himself through his own legislative will: it is because they are imposed on the Leibnizian agent as part of the very order of things in which he exists that they may seem to pose some threat to the reality of his independence.

Little has been said so far about the type of conduct which the moral necessities enjoin. Rescher has written that Leibniz's ethics merely support 'certain standard traditional views' (*III*, 147), but it can be argued they are, at least to some extent, neither standard nor traditional in seventeenth-century terms. For instance, although many moral philosophers had naturally regarded benevolence as a moral virtue, very few of them had given *active* benevolence the central role that it plays for Leibniz : they had thought of it more in terms of sentiment. Neither had they laid the same emphasis upon seeking the welfare of others *as an end*, or even managed to account for its possibility in terms of the egoistic theory of volition they shared with Leibniz, a fact that is greatly to his credit. This may even be regarded as one of his most significant theories, inasmuch as it anticipates the notion of a 'kingdom of ends' that formed such an important part of Kantian ethics. Leibniz's views prescribe a life of practical morality above all, a wholehearted and sincere attempt to benefit other people in accordance with the precepts of natural justice. Contemplation, sentiment and affection play a minimal part in all this, which is a significant departure even from the ethics of his contemporaries.

Despite this, it cannot really be maintained that Leibniz's system represents a significant contribution to moral philosophy. It is true that he has a number of important insights, as in his reconciliation of egoism and altruism, and that some of his theories provide an interesting approach to recurrent problems, of which his theory of duty is an example. Its real value, however, lies in the context of the history of thought. Leibniz was trained in the traditions of Scholastic philosophy, leavened by his reading of Plato and Aristotle; and thus we find that his theory conforms to the traditional model, in which moral conduct is represented as the means to happiness. At the same time it is the theory from which Kant broke away, for though few of Leibniz's works were published until long after his death, the main structure of his philosophy was enshrined in the popular works of Christian Wolff (*30*). Accordingly, one also finds many points at which it anticipates the later mode of moral philosophy. Leibniz's moral system, in fact, is the most sophisticated example of the traditional ethics that one is able to find. It is extensive and complete, dealing with all aspects of the moral life and relating them intelligibly to one another. It is coherent, forming a close-knit system of theories developed from a few simple concepts, and leaving remarkably few points at which tension or contradiction can be discerned. It is intimately connected with a larger system of philosophy, linking with metaphysics on the one hand, and with theology and political science on the other. And especially in its underlying theory of value it 'brings [morality] before the court of pure reason', as Kant put it (K.IV. 443), permitting the *a priori* deduction of moral truth that he was later to pursue, and therein transcending the tradition of moral philosophy from which it was developed.

Bibliography

(A) WORKS CITED BY ABBREVIATION

(I) TEXTS OF LEIBNIZ

A = Preussisches Akademie der Wissenschaften: *G. W. Leibniz, Sämtliche Schriften und Briefe*. Berlin, 1923–

BH = Bodemann, E.: *Die Leibniz-Handschriften in der königlichen öffentlichen Bibliothek zu Hannover*. Hildesheim, 1966

C = Couturat, L.: *Opuscules et fragments inédits de Leibniz*. Paris, 1903

D = Dutens, L.: *G. G. Leibnitii opera omnia* . . . Geneva, 1768

E = Erdmann, J. E.: *G. G. Leibnitii opera philosophica quae exstant* . . . Berlin, 1839

G = Gerhardt, C. I.: *Die philosophischen Schriften von G. W. Leibniz*. Halle, 1860

Gr = Grua, G.: *G. W. Leibniz – Textes inédits*. Paris, 1948

Gu = Guhrauer, G. E.: *Leibniz' deutsche Schriften*. Berlin, 1838

GW = Gerhardt, C. I.: *Briefwechsel zwischen Leibniz und Christian Wolf*. Halle, 1860

M = Mollat, G.: *Rechtphilosophisches aus Leibnizens ungedruckten Schriften*. Leipzig, 1885

NL = Foucher de Careil, A.: *G. W. Leibniz – Nouvelles lettres et opuscules inédits*. Paris, 1857

OH = Feller, J. F.: *Otium Hanoveranum, sive miscellanea ex ore et schedis illustris viri G. G. Leibnitii* . . . Leipzig, 1718

RI = Foucher de Careil, A.: *Refutation inédite de Spinoza par Leibniz*. Paris, 1854

(II) OTHER TEXTS

AT = Descartes, R.: *Œuvres*, publiées par C. Adam et P. Tannery. Paris, 1897

EN = Aristotle: *Ethica Nicomachea*, ed. L. Bywater. Oxford, 1962

K = Kant, I.: *Gesammelte Schriften*, herausgegeben von der

königlich Preussischen Akademie der Wissenschaften. Berlin, 1902–

R = Raphael, D. D.: *British Moralists 1650–1800*. Oxford 1969 (cited by paragraph, not page)

S = Spinoza, B. de: *Opera, quotquot reperta sunt*, ed. J. Van Vloten and J. P. N. Land. The Hague, 1895

SP = Aquinas, St Thomas: *De veritate catholicae fidei contra gentiles, seu summa philosophica*. Nemausi, 1853

ST = Aquinas, St Thomas: *Summa theologiae* – text and translation ed. T. Gilby. London, 1964–

(B) WORKS CITED BY NUMBER

(I) TEXTS OF LEIBNIZ

1. Belaval, Y.: *G. W. Leibniz, confessio philosophi*. Paris, 1961
2. Bodemann, E.: *Der Briefwechsel des G. W. Leibniz in der königlichen öffentlichen Bibliothek zu Hannover*. Hildesheim, 1966
3. Emery, J-A.: *Esprit de Leibniz, ou receuil de pensées choisies sur la religion, la morale*, etc. Lyon, 1772
4. Gerhardt, C. I.: *Leibnizens mathematische Schriften*. Berlin, 1849
5. Klopp, O.: *Die Werke von Leibniz* . . . (erste Reihe). Hannover, 1864
6. Schrecker, P.: *G. W. Leibniz, lettres et fragments inédits* . . . Paris, 1934

(II) OTHER TEXTS

7. Aquinas, Thomas: *De ente et essentia*, ed. C. Capelle. Paris, 1956
8. Aristotle: *Categories*, ed. Paluello. Oxford, 1949
9. Aristotle: *Physica*, ed. W. D. Ross. Oxford, 1955
10. Aristotle: *Metaphysica*, ed. Ross. Oxford, 1958
11. Aristotle: *De Anima*, ed. Ross. Oxford, 1961
12. Augustine, St: *Œuvres* (Bibl. Augustin). Paris, 1941–
13. Butler, J.: *Works*, ed. Bernard. London, 1900
14. Cicero, M. T.: *De officiis libri tres*, ed. Holden. Cambridge, 1886
15. Cicero, M. T.: *De re publica*, ed. Ziegler. Leipzig, 1955

16. Condillac, E. B.: *Traité des systèmes*. Paris, 1749
17. Conway, Anne: *Principia philosophiae* . . . Amsterdam, 1690
18. Grotius, H.: *De iure belli ac pacis*. Amsterdam, 1712
19. Hobbes, T.: *English works*, ed. Molesworth. London, 1839
20. Hobbes, T.: *Opera philosophica*, ed. Molesworth. London, 1839
21. Houtteville, C. F.: *La religion chrétienne* . . . Paris, 1740
22. Justinian: *Institutiones* and *Digesta*, in *Corpus iuris civilis*, vol. I. Berlin, 1882
23. Locke, J.: *Essay concerning human understanding*, ed. Yolton. London, 1967
24. Norris, J.: *The theory and regulation of love*. London, 1694
25. Plato: *Opera*, ed. Burnet. Oxford, 1967
26. Porphyry: *Opuscula selecta*, ed. Nauck. Leipzig, 1886
27. Pufendorf, S.: *Les devoirs de l'homme et du citoyen* . . . (*avec le jugement de Leibniz*) . . . Amsterdam, 1735
28. Seneca: *Dialogues*, ed. Bourgery, vol. 2. Paris, 1955
29. Thomasius, J.: *Philosophia practica* . . . Leipzig, 1679
30. Wolff, C.: *Philosophia practica universalis*. Leipzig, 1738

(III) BIBLIOGRAPHIES

31. Müller, K.: *Leibniz-Bibliographie*. Frankfurt, 1967
32. Müller, K. and Krönert, G.: *Leben und Werk von G. W. Leibniz*. Frankfurt, 1969
33. Ravier, E.: *Bibliographie des œuvres de Leibniz*. Paris, 1937
34. Schrecker, P.: 'Une bibliographie de Leibniz'. *Revue Philos.*, 1938

(IV) SELECTED SECONDARY WORKS

35. Abraham, W. E.: 'Complete concepts and Leibniz' distinction between necessary and contingent propositions'. *Studia Leibnitiana*, 1969
36. Abraham, W. E.: 'The incompatibility of individuals'. *Nous*, 1972
37. Ahern, M. B.: *The problem of evil*. London, 1971
38. Baier, K.: 'Moral obligation'. *Am. Philos. Q.*, 1966
39. Barber, W. H.: *Leibniz in France – a study in French reactions to Leibnizianism 1670–1760*. Oxford, 1955
40. Baruzi, J.: *Leibniz et l'organization religieuse de la terre*. Paris, 1907

41. Baynes, N. H.: *The political ideas of St Augustine's 'De Civitate Dei'* (Historical Ass. Pamphlet 104). London, 1936

42. Beck, L. W.: *Early German philosophy, Kant and his predecessors.* Cambridge (Mass.), 1969

43. Belaval, Y.: *Leibniz' critique de Descartes.* Paris, 1960

44. Belaval, Y.: 'Le problème de l'erreur chez Leibniz'. *Zeitschrift für philos. Forsch.*, 1966

45. Bird, O. A.: *The idea of justice.* New York, 1967

46. Bouillet, M-N.: *Les Ennéades de Plotin.* Paris, 1857

47. Broad, C. D.: *Five types of ethical theory.* London, 1934

48. Carr, H. W.: *Leibniz.* New York, 1960

49. Cassirer, E.: *Die platonische Renaissance in England . . .* Berlin, 1932

50. Chauvin, E. (Stephanus): *Lexicon rationale . . .* Rotterdam, 1692

51. Couturat, L.: *La logique de Leibniz . . .* Paris, 1901

52. Dewey, J.: 'Leibniz's New Essays – a critical exposition', in *The early works of John Dewey*, vol. 1, ed. S. Illinois Univ. Carbondale, 1969

53. *Dictionnaire de théologie Catholique.* Paris, 1923–

54. Feinberg, J. (ed.): *Moral concepts.* Oxford, 1969

55. Fontenelle, B.: 'Eloge de Leibniz', in *Histoire de l'Academie Royale des Sciences de Paris*, 1716

56. Foucher de Careil, A.: *Leibniz, Descartes et Spinoza.* Paris, 1862

57. Frankfurt, H. G. (ed.): *Leibniz – a collection of critical essays.* New York, 1972

58. Friedmann, G.: 'Leibniz et Spinoza – les intentions morales des systèmes . . .' *Rev. Philos. de France*, 1945

59. Friedmann, G.: *Leibniz et Spinoza.* Paris, 1946

60. Friedrich, C. J.: *The philosophy of law . . .* Chicago, 1963

61. Gardiner, P. L.: 'Pain and evil'. *Aristotelian Soc. Supplement*, 1964

62. Gilson, E.: *Index scolastico-cartesien.* Paris, 1913 (cited by paragraph, not page)

63. Gilson, E.: *Le Thomisme.* Paris, 1922

64. Grua, G.: 'Optimisme et piété Leibnizienne avant 1686. ..' *Rev. Philos. de France*, 1946

65. Grua, G.: *Jurisprudence universelle et théodicée selon Leibniz*. Paris, 1953
66. Grua, G.: *La justice humaine selon Leibniz*. Paris, 1956
67. Hannequin, A.: *Quae fuerit prior Leibnitii philosophia* . . . Paris, 1895. (Also in French translation, in *Etudes d'histoire des sciences* . . . Paris, 1908.)
68. Hazo, R. G.: *The idea of love*. New York, 1967
69. Heinekamp, A.: 'Zu den Begriffen realitas . . .' *Studia Leibnitiana Suppl.* 1
70. Heinekamp, A.: 'Das Problem des Guten bei Leibniz'. *Kantstudien* Ergänz 98, 1969
71. Hicks, R. D.: *Stoic and Epicurean*. London, 1910
72. Hohfeld, W. N.: *Fundamental legal conceptions* . . . New Haven, 1964
73. Hook, S. (ed.): *Law and philosophy, a symposium*. New York, 1964
74. Hostler, J. M.: 'Some remarks on "omne possibile exigit existere" '. *Studia Leibnitiana*, 1973
75. Hudson, W. D. (ed.): *The is-ought question* . . . London, 1969
76. Ishiguro, H.: *Leibniz's philosophy of logic and language*. London, 1972
77. Jalabert, J.: 'La psychologie de Leibniz'. *Rev. Philos. de France*, 1946
78. Jalabert, J.: *Le dieu de Leibniz*. Paris, 1960
79. Jalabert, J.: 'Création et harmonie preétablie selon Leibniz'. *Studia Leibnitiana*, 1971
80. Johnson, O. A.: 'Human freedom in the best of all possible worlds'. *Philos. Q.*, 1954
81. Jordan, G. J.: *The reunion of the churches* . . . London, 1927
82. Keller, L.: *G. W. Leibniz und die deutschen Sozietäten des 17 Jahrhunderts*. Berlin, 1903
83. Kenny, A.: 'Descartes on the will', in *Cartesian Studies*, ed. R. J. Butler. Oxford, 1972
84. Kors, J-B.: *La justice primitive et le péché originel d'après St Thomas*. (Bibl. Thomiste, vol. 2.) Paris, 1930
85. Latta, R.: *Leibniz – the Monadology* . . . Oxford, 1898
86. Le Chevallier, L.: *La morale de Leibniz*. Paris, 1933
87. Leibniz-Kongress, 2nd International. (References are to

papers delivered – probably to be published in supplements to *Studia Leibnitiana*.)

88. Lieder, F. W. C.: 'Friedrich Spee and the Theodicy of Leibniz'. *J. Eng. & Gn. Philology*, 1912

89. Lovejoy, A. O.: 'Optimism and romanticism'. *PMLA*, 1927

90. Lovejoy, A. O.: *The great chain of being* . . . Cambridge (Mass.), 1936

91. Macdonell, J. and Manson, E.: *Great jurists of the world.* London, 1913

92. MacIntyre, A.: 'Pleasure as a reason for action'. *The Monist*, 1965

93. Mackie, J. L.: 'Evil and omnipotence'. *Mind*, 1958

94. Maritain, J.: *Moral philosophy* (vol. 1). London, 1964

95. Matter, M.: *Le mysticisme en France au temps de Fénelon.* Paris, 1865

96. McCloskey, H. J.: 'The problem of evil'. *J. Bible & Religion*, 1962

97. McGill, V. J.: *The idea of happiness.* New York, 1967

98. Memmo, P. E.: *Giordano Bruno's 'The Heroic Frenzies'.* Ann Arbor, 1961

99. Moore, G. E.: *Principia ethica.* Cambridge, 1903

100. Mulvaney, R. J.: 'The early development of Leibniz's concept of justice'. *J. Hist. Ideas*, 1968

101. Naert, E.: *Mémoire et conscience de soi selon Leibniz.* Paris, 1961

102. Naert, E.: *La pensée politique de Leibniz.* Paris, 1964

103. Parkinson, G. H. R.: *Logic and reality in Leibniz's metaphysics.* Oxford, 1965

104. Parkinson, G. H. R.: 'Leibniz on human freedom'. *Studia Leibnitiana* Sonderheft II.

105. Passmore, J.: *The perfectibility of man.* London, 1970

106. Patrides, C. A.: *The Cambridge Platonists.* London, 1969

107. Politella, J.: *Platonism, Aristotelianism and Cabalism in the philosophy of Leibniz.* Philadelphia, 1938

108. Raphael, D. D. (ed.): *Political theory and the rights of man.* London, 1967

109. Rawls, J.: *A theory of justice.* Oxford, 1972

110. Reiss, H. (ed.): *Kant's political writings.* Cambridge, 1970

111. Rescher, N.: *The philosophy of Leibniz*. Englewood Cliffs, 1967
112. Rescher, N.: *Essays in philosophical analysis*. Pittsburgh 1969
113. Riley, P.: *The political writings of Leibniz*. Cambridge, 1972
114. Rodis-Lewis, G.: *La morale de Descartes*. Paris, 1957
115. Russell, B. A. W.: *A critical exposition of the philosophy of Leibniz*. Cambridge, 1900 (cited by paragraph, not page)
116. Russell, L. J.: 'Leibniz'. *Philosophy*, 1936
117. Ryle, G.: *The concept of mind*. Harmondsworth, 1963
118. Schiedermair, H.: 'Das Phänomen der Macht und die Idee des Rechts bei G. W. Leibniz'. *Studia Leibnitiana* Suppl. VII
119. Schilpp, P. A.: *Kant's pre-critical ethics*. Evanston, 1938
120. Schneider, H-P.: *Iustitia Universalis . . .* Frankfurt, 1967
121. Schneiders, W.: 'Naturrecht und Gerechtigkeit bei Leibniz'. *Zeitschrift für Philos. Forsch.*, 1966
122. Schrecker, P.: 'Leibniz – ses idées sur l'organization des relations internationales'. *Proc. Brit. Acad.*, 1937. (In English, *J. Hist. Ideas*, 1946)
123. Schrecker, P.: 'Leibniz and the Timaeus'. *Rev. of Metaph.*, 1950
124. Trendelenburg, F. A.: *Historische Beiträge zur Philosophie* (vol. 2). Berlin, 1855
125. Vleeschauwer, H. J.: *G. W. Leibniz – Vader van die moderne Universiteit*. Pretoria (S. Africa), 1967
126. Voltaire, F. M. A.: *Candide*, ed. Taylor. Oxford, 1962
127. Von Wright, G. H.: *Norm and action . . .* London, 1963
128. Von Wright, G. H.: *The varieties of goodness*. London, 1963
129. Walker, D. P.: *The decline of Hell . . .* London, 1964
130. Ward, A. W.: *Leibniz as a politician*. Manchester, 1911
131. Warrender, H.: *The political theory of Hobbes . . .* Oxford, 1961
132. Wood, A. W.: *Kant's moral religion*. Ithaca (N.Y.), 1970

Index